DOVILE RIEBSCHLAGER

LUXURY OF THE NEW ERA

A NEW VISION OF THE FASHION WORLD

THE BOSS BOOKS

LUXURY OF THE NEW ERA
Dovile Riebschlager

Edited and published by: The Boss Books/Libri d'Impresa Edizioni

One Hour Marketing Srl
via Alessandro Volta 34, 20825 Barlassina (MB), Italy

www.thebossbooks.com

Printed in January 2023
Copyright @ 2023 Dovile Riebschlager

All rights reserved. This book or parts thereof may not be reproduced or transmitted in any form by any means – electronic, mechanical, photocopy, recording, or otherwise – without prior written permission of the author.

ISBN 9791280622747

CONTENTS

Introduction: The old vs. new way for luxury fashion — 5

Chapter 1: The backlash of fast fashion — 15

Chapter 2: Fabrics: long-lasting and pleasurable — 29

Chapter 3: Textile production reimagined — 57

Chapter 4: Reinventing shipping solutions — 75

Chapter 5: New standards in couture design — 95

Chapter 6: Breaking the cycle in fashion shows — 123

Chapter 7: The energy of clothes on the consumer — 145

Chapter 8: How fashion can nurture your uniqueness — 167

Acknowledgments — 187

References — 191

What is the New Era of luxury in fashion? — 203

Dovile Riebschlager — 207

INTRODUCTION

I would like to start off by applauding you for reading this book. Your courage and initiative to find out what is truly going on in our fashion industry nowadays means that you care deeply about the impact it will have on our world today as well as on generations to come.

I can tell that you either have a deep appreciation for fashion or you are engaged in a career in the fashion industry.
Either way, you feel there is an urgent need for an awakening that needs to happen in our current fashion system/world and that it can no longer operate the way it has been for decades.
The world as we know it now, post-Covid era, has been shifting at a rapid pace and with that comes a paradigm shift.
The fashion industry is no longer immune and will need to embrace change if it is going to survive as well as thrive in the future.

Are you a fashion aficionado? Are you the parent of a teen who is struggling to give him/her the best quality clothes? Are you a fashion expert in the field working tirelessly with your sleeves rolled up doing the hard work, and eager to find out a solution to some of the pressing challenges that this industry is facing?
Well, the truth is you are not alone. I have written this book with you in mind.

I admire your dedication and desire to uncover the truth, searching for new unchartered ways of moving into an era where fashion can retain its luxurious, glamorous status, yet can go beyond all the sustainability talk that has been emerging lately. It will need to be reconfigured and adapted to a new world - the rise of new way of luxury fashion where the betterment of society is also rewarded alongside luxury and sustainability.

Now more than ever we are in need of change agents from the buyer all the way to the designer, as well as the production/manufacturing side of the equation. This is a collective effort. I will be honest with you, it does require gaining a deeper knowledge of how and why the system is no longer working, and on the flip side, I can say the future of fashion is bright and that I see each one of you as powerful protagonists in its advancement.

Know that a significant power lies in the hands of people like you who make the purchase - you are choosing the system which you would like to support and ultimately you are the one who can change an outworn, out of date system.

Here are a few reasons why I have written this book for you:

- Because you deserve much more than just sustainable clothes. You deserve also the best quality. Why should you be accepting something so crappy and cheaply made that is ultimately affecting your skin and health? Quality should be a luxurious and glamorous experience as well as good for humanity and saving our planet.

FOREWORD

- Due to super-fast production, designs are generally not well stress-tested before sale. Modern clothing is not made to last. After a few uses, it is tossed in the landfill. In this post-COVID era, with work requirements having shifted so dramatically, you might be one of the many who doesn't go into the office everyday. With that, you probably might not need as many clothes and can afford to have less yet invest in higher quality. Aren't you dreaming of finally owning more luxurious clothes that have longevity written all over them? Are you perhaps one of the countless individuals who is tired of buying and throwing clothes away after a few washes? Actually, you probably are spending more in the long run when you compare it to owning a few higher quality clothes that might initially make you feel like you're spending a lot of money.

- Additionally, you have the power to stop the negative impact that cutting corners on quality has had on humanity and our future generations. Maybe you have been searching for ways to support a worthy cause but nothing so far has captured your interest. There is no need to feel overwhelmed that, to be of value, you will need to spend countless hours volunteering your time in order to be of service. You can be a change agent with the least effort from the comfort of your home whether online or in person and you can make impactful changes as a buyer or a designer. I am going to show you how in the upcoming chapters.

On the following pages, I will be sharing with you the knowledge I have acquired after decades of trial and error in what might be perceived as a successful career in fashion design. And, I can say along the way, there have been some challenging lessons I have had to learn. From that moment some successful solutions have emerged and I want to not only inspire you, but also give you concrete tools and practical steps you can follow. I call it the new way of luxury fashion.

What I am going to share is going to give you the needed power and support in order to start implementing them in your buying habits or in ways to conduct business as a designer/producer from boutiques all the way to major department stores.

I have been working in the fashion industry for what seems like an eternity. I have had the privilege of seeing the fashion world from different vantage points that the majority of the people never had the chance to see. I feel this responsibility to open you up to the fashion world in ways that have never been done before. To show you both the good and the not so great sides of the fashion industry and what goes on behind the scenes.

I never acquired a proper fashion designer education. The way I started learning about fabrics was back in my home country of Lithuania (which was under Communist rule at the time) working in a factory producing synthetic material around the late 1980s and early 1990s.
My eyes were opened to some shocking truths about the process.

FOREWORD

I vividly remember to this day the way water was used and the foul smell of the dirty water from washing the fabric. This factory weaved the fabric and printed it.

They had to wash the fabric multiple times and the amount of water waste was incredible; so much water usage plus the very specific chemical smell. The remnants of it can be traced to the fabric stores, where synthetic silks still have a faint unmistakable smell of synthetic dyes. When you dye the fabric, it needs to be soaked, rinsed, steamed, and the dirty water secretes a quite unpleasant odor. I never had any health issues or any allergic reaction in my life until I passed the room where they kept the synthetic dyes.

As I went by the room, I started choking and did not understand why or what was happening to me. From my textile chemical engineering studies I knew that the dye is composed of a fine powder: a highly toxic chemical compound.

You can use natural dyes for natural fabrics but because synthetic fabrics are sleek/slippery and nothing sticks to them, you need a dye that is chemical and harsh in nature to do the work. Furthermore, reactive dyes are used with the fabric because a more aggressive process is needed for synthetic fabrics.

I recall to this day my severe reaction, I know that if I had worked with dyes and not produced screens for screen printing, I would have had severe health problems.

This only strengthened my desire to study textile as art as I just wanted to escape this dreary environment.

To this day, I still cannot pinpoint the exact time when I first fell in love with fashion design, but it was really early. By nine I was creating paper dolls and the maker of their exuberant outfits, selling them to my classmates for the price of a cinnamon bun.

While other children were waiting for animations on TV, I was glued to TV watching runway shows from Paris, a very rare occurrence for kids my age.

In my teenage years I realized I was able to transform my appearance with clothes, accessories and makeup. I started sewing when I was thirteen.
I got tired of waiting for my mom to finish my clothes and asked her to show me how the sewing machine works. That was magic, I still remember the first dress I made for myself.

Despite my disastrous short-lived job at the factory, fashion was still in my blood. Fashion kept calling. It is my life. I never did get the proper fashion designer education, but I do have several degrees in Textiles Engineering and Art.

In the mid-90s, my life attracted amazing opportunities to test me as a fashion designer. For a while, I was creating stage costumes for my friend, a ballet dancer, and her troupe.

FOREWORD

When I first tried my hand at fashion designs commercially, I sold a children's FW95 collection to one of the biggest Lithuanian apparel factories, the same year my first runway collection was accepted at the fashion show "Woman and Fashion" juried by French fashion experts.
It was a big deal, but the collection was never finished, because I doubted my skill and entrusted sewing to a professional seamstress. Everything was going my way, but I decided to postpone it all and move to Chicago to learn English.

I have been blessed to have been exposed to working under more dire conditions in my country of Lithuania all the way to designing clothes on the runways for US fashions shows including our prestigious New York Fashion Week.

When I work on new designs, I feel alive, I can finally breathe. I cannot honestly say how I create, to me it feels like it just happens. Sometimes it's a dream, sometimes I see a fabric and design just pops in my head.

The fashion world has given me so much and I have been truly blessed even with the challenges that have come along the way. It gave me the possibility to express myself, to generate creation, to always be pushed to think out of the box.

My heart overflows with gratitude and there is nothing more fulfilling than when I hear some of my customers tell me something like 'the fabrics you've selected are absolutely divine'.

Where do they come from? I've never experienced anything like it. Despite my immense passion and love for fashion, I am still not wearing rose tinted glasses.
What keeps me up at night is the sense of responsibility, that I feel towards each and every consumer out there as well as towards the designers, to expose the not so pleasant aspects we are all somehow aware of, but that are probably getting swept under the rug: the not so glamorous issues.

Starting from the sustainability of the production today all the way to featuring skinny models in fashion shows that are advocating anorexia, as well as the advertising/marketing constantly encouraging buying more and more with no end in sight.
And, the list goes on.

This book is not about publishing one more of the hundreds of books out there complaining about the world and saying that fashion is not sustainable.
Nowadays, we are bombarded with that.
Go into any bookshop and you can read all about sustainability problems as well as how the fashion system is broken.

What I want to do is provide solutions in a way that benefits all involved, from the the factory worker in the production all the way to you, the consumer.
The foundation needs to be fixed and you are part of the solution.
Humanity's future and the planet are in peril.
It is time to make the change.

FOREWORD

Let's work together in the vision of a new era for the fashion world: glamorous and sustainable.
This is the new frontier of fashion and desirability

One that goes beyond sustainable pleasure. I call it sustainable luxury. How will a sustainable luxury that works for the better good of all look like? Keep reading to find out. I am going to unfold a new, healthier way.

Chapter 1
THE BACKLASH OF FAST FASHION

"What I show on the runway is the extent of my imagination and skill, but when I work with my clients, I listen, because it is not what I want, but what we create together."

DOVILE RIEBSCHLAGER

1. THE BACKLASH OF FAST FASHION

Recently, I was flying to Hawaii for a fashion runway show and I had the chance to look out of the plane at the Pacific Ocean. With a confused look on my face, I wondered, why are there so many ships in the ocean and what are they doing, you know, somewhere relatively so far from the mainland.

One of the models, who had a better view, took a picture and we magnified that photo. With shock I realized it was garbage. The Hawaiian Islands are surrounded by a sea of garbage. The magnitude of this devastating impact on our planet is mind-blowing and we have no idea of the severity of this environmental issue that is ultimately going to destroy our planet. If we wait any longer the damage will be irreversible.

Fast fashion that goes hand in hand with fast production is a contributing factor in the negative environmental impact we are currently witnessing.

FAST FASHION DEFINED

In the 1990s, fast fashion emerged. That is when Zara opened their doors in New York. The New York Times described Zara's ultra-quick production model as "fast fashion".

"Every week there's a new shipment from Spain," said Juan Lopez, the head of Zara's United States operation. "The stock in the store changes every three weeks. The latest trend is what we're after.

It takes 15 days between a new idea and getting it into the stores."¹

Following in the footsteps of Zara were stores like Forever 21 and H&M that also minimized their lead times between design and retail delivery to just two weeks.

What happened to the days when we followed a practical mindset of just acquiring what we needed? If we want to break it down further, all we truly need are clothes for the warm and cool seasons. To be fashionable and to keep up with the trends, everyone is thinking in seasons, of which there are four. The question is do you need to have a design for every season and does it need to change every single year? For the sake of practicality and simplifying the consumer purchasing process, only two seasons should be considered: summer and fall.

In the fast fashion world where making sales is the life blood of the business, retailers have been known to push for fifty-two style seasons every year. What does that mean for you the buyer? Excessive spending. Even if you feel like you are saving money with more yet cheaper clothes. It is all about "staying trendy" and that requires a whole new wardrobe every week. This is probably a winning formula for great retailers and fashion brands, however, it's a huge fashion *faux pas* for our environment. Furthermore, sales people in the US get paid per hour and then they get an additional commission on what they sell. Then, it becomes like a pressure to succeed and pushing past the goals for the month. Salespeople just want you to buy more. From personal experience during my visits to stores, they kept pushing products for me to try on and kept complimenting me saying how amazing, and great I looked in the outfits, even when they looked like crap. I would come home and then think why did I buy that. I was so enamored by the way the salesperson had hyped the product and felt so flattered, that I did not realize it was not done with the truest of intentions for my benefit but rather for profit. Honesty and truthfulness have been blatantly disregarded in the name of money and getting everything done faster. Fast fashion is no longer working. Fashion should be based on what is good and will work for you. It is evident that the foundation of fast fashion is crumbling.

The Cost of Cheaply Priced Clothes

As fast fashion built momentum, it began to include a few other not so desirable aspects: super cheap prices and a devaluation of clothes.

Before the emergence of $5 T-shirts and BOGO sales on every attire imaginable, people had a much greater appreciation for garments and the fabric. Some of you may remember that in decades prior, Home Economics class in high school used to offer classes on the art of learning how to sew. Parents used to know and teach their kids the skills required to mend a rip, check a seam, and replace a button. Above all, we prioritized durability and high-quality materials. Bring in the fast fashion and all this went out the window. Cheap, plastic-based fabrics became the highlight of our wardrobes. We became accepting of tears, and we viewed it from a different perspective. Ditch spending the time worrying about an unraveling seam (and forget about trying to fix it!) when you could just replace that jacket with a new, trendier version — and at a price that doesn't break the bank? Mindset being: wow, truly a win-win for me — I get a new and better version. Or, at least that is what you were led to believe by the fashion industry — everything is disposable and there is more of it out there, so feel free to toss that jacket into the wastebasket. Consumers choosing quantity over quality has become the dangerous norm. Have you heard of the saying that too much of a "good" thing can be bad, and to go with that is also that too much of a thing with hidden costs can also prove to be *really* detrimental? In early 2000's, I saw $9 jeans in Old Navy and my mind exploded, how can it be? Before it reached the shelf the fabric had to be produced, someone had to design, sew it, transport it and everyone had to have a profit of it. I had no idea about fast fashion industry, but common sense was ringing bells in my mind.

Hidden costs means that the global fashion industry remains riddled with human rights abuses and environmental degradation. Supply chains remain complex, fragmented, deregulated and opaque. A lack of visibility of supply chains can allow exploitative, unsafe working conditions and environmental damage to thrive while obscuring who has the responsibility and power to redress these issues.

According to Fashion Revolution Foundation's 2021, that recently released a report, transparency is foundational to achieving systemic change in the global fashion industry. Transparency is not to be confused with sustainability. However, without transparency, achieving

1. THE BACKLASH OF FAST FASHION

a sustainable, accountable, and fair fashion industry will be impossible. It is my hope that this book not only unveils the unglamorous side of the fashion industry, but also propels you to take action towards a new way of sustainable, luxury fashion.

I am a huge advocate of transparency underpinning transformative change, but unfortunately much of the fashion value chain remains opaque, while human and environmental exploitation thrives with impunity.

A lack of transparency perpetuates an exclusive system, where people are expected to trust brands who have continued to put profit and growth above all else. When brands publicly disclose information, anyone is allowed to scrutinize their policies, hold them accountable for their claims and advocate for positive change.

Transparency is only the beginning stage in a process to taking action towards lasting change. There is an obligation and a responsibility to buyers and the planet to be transparent, so the truth can set you free to choose a higher road in your purchasing/spending habits that will ultimately benefit you and the Earth.

NEGATIVE IMPACTS OF PRODUCTION AND CONSUMPTION:

Textile Waste

A study by Greenpeace estimates that $500 billion are lost each year due to consumers tossing out their clothing after wearing them a few times and failing to recycle them. In another report, McKinsey estimates that since 2000 the number of garments being produced have doubled. Not to mention that we are only keeping clothing for only about half as long as we did at the turn of the century. Sadly enough in some cases we are discarding garments after just seven or eight wears! Truly a recipe for disaster!

Did you know that that the U.S. throws away up to 11.3 million tons of textile waste each year—around 2,150 pieces of clothing each second? The numbers are staggering and hard to wrap your mind around. Studies show that UK consumers (one in three respondents) consider clothes old after one or two wears.

Carbon Emissions, Water Use and Pollution

When it comes to the morality of the fashion industry, numbers speak for themselves. As the second most polluting industry on the planet – exceeded only by oil production – fashion has a lot to answer for. Climate crisis and the human misery it creates in turn is the price we are increasingly paying for our thirst for what's new, now and in the future.

Water use and pollution also take place during clothing production. About 20 percent of industrial water pollution is due to garment manufacturing, while the world uses 5 trillion liters (1.3 trillion gallons) of water each year for fabric dyeing alone, enough to fill 2 million Olympic-sized swimming pools.

Cotton is considered to be one of the greatest offenders when it comes to water consumption. Just one cotton T-shirt requires 2,700 liters of water. That happens to be the amount an average person drinks in two-and-a-half years.

Uncovered: The Dirty Secret of Exploitative Labor Practices

Beyond the environmental impact, fast fashion has a huge responsibility when it comes to advocating exploitative labor practices and needs to be addressed. Child labor, forced labor, insane work hours, abysmal pay, and exposure to toxic chemicals are what makes that $10 dress a reality.

Let us not forget about the tragic Rana Plaza disaster in 2013—that killed more than 1,132 textile workers in Bangladesh. The majority of them were girls and some of them had complained about cracks in the walls in the days before the collapse.

When we look at clothing, we may just see the price tag. But it's important to realize the amount of missing information that underlies it all—the environmental and human costs that made it possible for you to wear that garment.

REASONS WHY FAST FASHION BRANDS ALLOW SUCH PRACTICES

To keep clothes at ultra low prices, fast fashion brands need their costs to be low. One of the main ways of doing this is to drive down the wages of garment workers in the supply chain.

Fashion brands have "chased the cheap needle" around the world, seeking countries with the lowest labor standards, so that garment workers can be easily exploited. In recent years, many US fast fashion brands due to the "backlash against globalism and the accompanying protectionists call to buy American", have found the cheap needle closer to home, often in quasi-legal factories and domestic sweatshops. One can find these sub-standard facilities predominantly in cities such as Los Angeles and New York. Seen more often in Los Angeles because of the huge undocumented immigrant population. In an investigation conducted by the UCLA Labor Center, 72 percent of Los Angeles garment workers stated that factories were dirty; 60 percent said they were poorly ventilated and led to respiratory ailments; 47 percent reported disgusting restrooms; and 42 percent said they had seen rats. According to the investigation, the brands allegedly producing in such conditions included Forever 21, Wet Seal, Papaya, and Charlotte Russe.

Worker exploitation is an essential part of the fast fashion model. As a buyer, having this knowledge means power, as now you can choose to purchase from a different source where ethics and quality are valued.

1. THE BACKLASH OF FAST FASHION

Next time you step into the store, if the item is cheap, chances are that the person who produced it was paid little and most likely went through significant physical hardship.

"The transition to change the way it works is too slow," says Dr. Rima Trofimovaite, Head of Certification for Planet Mark, a sustainability certification that aims to help companies strengthen their environmental strategies. "Without immediate action, the fashion industry will fail to meet the global targets set in the Paris Agreement, limiting global warming to 1.5 °C. And as in any business, legislators and consumers are the most powerful drivers for change. It is in consumers' hands to drive the change to a more sustainable fashion industry."

"It is critical that consumers can identify which businesses have adopted authentic sustainable practices through transparency, from the manufacturing process to marketing. The fashion industry needs to shift from linear to circular product lifecycle models and there is a lot of work that needs to be done to achieve that. This shift in manufacturing model would support conscious customers, increase efficiency and result in significant financial gain," adds Dr. Trofimovaite.

What is the Alternative to Fast Fashion?

Up to this point, you have been equipped with all the knowledge and awareness of all the negative impacts of fast fashion.

If you have read this far, you are probably asking what is it that you can do to be an agent of change. For the consumer, it will be a matter of where and how you will be doing your shopping next.

As for both the seasoned and novice designers out there, the question will be how can I select better quality fabrics as well as choose ethical production processes moving forward. It is my hope that by the time you have finished reading this book, you will have a clear map of the actions you can employ right away.

The new way of sustainable, luxury fashion that is also the "slow fashion revolution". The new fashion era is here and I hope you are ready to dive in!

KEY POINTS

- In the next chapters, you will learn how fashionable clothing can be pleasurable and superior in quality as well as great for you the consumer, our planet and humanity.

- Quality should be your motivating factor rather than quantity.

- Don't let those fears that you are going to break the bank stop you from choosing higher quality clothing and craftsmanship. Employing the right method and shifting your purchasing habits can still be a win-win for you. It will be a lot more cost effective in the long run.

- Wearing clothes should not only be a luxurious pleasurable experience for you but also it needs to be ethical, sustainable and safeguard the well-being of your fellow earth citizens.

- Supporting the use of recycled or renewable materials is critical and it needs to be done in a way that is maintaining the glamour of fashion as well as its sustainability.

- Your changes will impact future generations to come and be a catalyst in a massive overhaul of a shaky fashion industry.

What motivates you to buy new clothes?
What brands dominate your closet?
Do you have a favorite label? What do you like about them?

Chapter 2
FABRICS: LONG-LASTING AND PLEASURABLE

2. FABRICS: LONG-LASTING AND PLEASURABLE

There is so much information out on the internet with regards to the dilemmas of fast fashion and its impact on the environment. Essentially, we are now immersed in a global fashion and environmental crisis. Despite the social media concern for ethical fashion and consumption, what I noticed is sorely lacking: a long-lasting equitable solution for all and generations to come. For every crisis there is a victory waiting to surface. Time is of the essence in finding the solution to the challenges the fashion industry is facing. As previously mentioned, whether you are a potential customer or a designer/manufacturer, you are part of the solution in this new way of sustainable, luxury fashion.

The new way of sustainable, ethical and luxury fashion begins with the fabric. Two questions you should start asking before purchasing anything is:

- Who made my clothes?
- What are my clothes made of?

So, let's begin by taking a deeper dive into the area of quality. According to SgT, a global team of quality management and manufacturing experts, "One of the main reasons why retail brands fail is because they've launched poor quality products that customers aren't willing to pay for. Some brands attempt to decrease manufacturing costs by skimping on raw material quality or first-class equipment which reduces the quality of products significantly. This is an enormous risk to take as already existing brands may lose valuable customer loyalty if products need to be recalled and brands starting out in the industry may miss their opportunity to make it.

The fourth industrial revolution's consumer is educated, sophisticated and quality conscious. They aren't interested in supporting brands that don't represent their image and style in terms of quality and sustainability.

Therefore, brands should ensure that quality is a priority and effective quality management processes should be implemented at every step of production. Brands should also consider outsourcing their quality management processes to textile quality specialists as there are many advantages involved."

For instance, let's take cotton. It is the oldest fabric known to man dating back to Egypt when they used to shroud mummies in a wrap made of cotton. One of the reasons cotton is so popular is because of its humidity absorbing qualities. At the same time, it is super comfortable, lightweight and — the best part for the consumer— it is cheap. Egypt has raised its production by 30% during 2021. Celebrating World Cotton Day on October 7, the Egyptian cabinet said "cotton cultivation and production have witnessed an increase compared to former years".

"The manufacture of cotton dates back to the 16th century. Handheld roller gins had been used in the Indian subcontinent since at earliest AD 500 and then in other regions.
The Indian worm-gear roller gin, invented sometime around the 16th century, has remained virtually unchanged up to the present time.

A modern mechanical cotton gin was created by American inventor Eli

2. FABRICS: LONG-LASTING AND PLEASURABLE

Whitney in 1793 and patented in 1794.

Whitney's gin used a combination of a wire screen and small wire hooks to pull the cotton through, while brushes continuously removed the loose cotton lint to prevent jams. It revolutionized the cotton industry in the United States, but also led to the growth of slavery in the American South. Whitney's gin made cotton farming more profitable, so plantation owners expanded their plantations and used more slaves to pick the cotton. If Whitney never invented a machine to harvest cotton, it still had to be picked by hand. The invention has thus been identified as an inadvertent contributing factor to the outbreak of the American Civil War."

The other thing is that cotton is native only to some region like Egypt and Central Asia. It is grown in desert type of lands, but the plant itself requires a lot of water.

When I was living in Lithuania, I managed to turn a blind eye to the Soviet Union's Rules of Conduct just to keep up with the increasing demand for cotton. A complete disregard for the ecological and social cost of cotton production.

Up until 1990 the country of Lithuania did not exist - it was known as the Lithuanian Soviet Republic and to call it Lithuania was considered a crime. There was absolutely no information available about any of the darker aspects of the country, so I couldn't turn blind eye on the things I wasn't aware of.
I recall when I was visiting Uzbekistan and saw these quite unattractive

cotton fields during wintertime and as a 16 year old I just thought how awful and ugly this looks. Only a decade later when Gorbachov's "glasnost" started I became aware of the horrible things happening in those fields.

I, too, probably unknowingly contributed to the success of cotton. The thing is we don't know what we don't know. As the saying goes hindsight is 20/20. We are now living in a rapidly growing digital age and information is instantly handed to us at the touch of a button. One can easily investigate and conduct research to see where and how everything is being sourced from food to clothes to the house you live in. The key is to be an active participant in your daily choices by independently investigating the truth for yourself. Knowledge is power. Reading this book is giving you invaluable insights as to how you can change your purchasing habits. If you are a designer/manufacturer, you, too, can change and improve your sourcing as well as production practices.

Going back to my earlier days growing up in Lithuania, I remember falling in love with cotton during my late teens. The Soviet world was not exactly fashion friendly. I felt out of sorts in that environment. I guess you could have called me a fashionista at that point. You could say I was a bit of a culture rebel. The only way around that system was that I knew how to sew which meant I could create my own clothes. At that time though I was just trying to not to drown in the sea of unremarkable sameness. Later, I realized that what I was doing was cultural rebellion.

2. FABRICS: LONG-LASTING AND PLEASURABLE

The turning point for me and the country came about during the late Soviet Era, as previously everything was scarce except for a short period. Suddenly, there was a global oil shortage and Russia was trading oil for a variety of imported products such as Italian cars, shoes, clothing from different countries as well as some other goods. A lot of interesting things and discoveries came about during this time.

That world was opened up to me when my mom had to go on frequent business trips to Moscow and St. Petersburg (Leningrad at that time); unfortunately I wasn't allowed on those trips under any circumstance as I had to go to school and moreover hotels most likely would not have allowed me even to stay there. The first time I was in Moscow during a school trip to Uzbekistan and witnessed that enormous line to get into GUM, as it was called the Glavnyj Universalnyj Magazin. GUM was perceived by the people as heaven on earth.

The majority of my mother's trips were to Moscow. The epitome of the Soviet Union was Moscow. Everything happened in Moscow. It was the heart and soul of everything: the best food, the best clothes, the best cars and so on. A funny side note about food: bananas were not available in most parts of the Soviet Union, yet I couldn't believe it, you could find all the bananas you could ever want there in the capital city of Moscow as well as meats and breads etc. People were flocking to Moscow in droves. Being only a young teenager at the time, I had a sense that access to Moscow was limited. Mainly for financial reasons, the unavailability of hotels and that you either had to be at work or in school. Etched in my memory was this market in front of the Red Square.

There were masses of people standing in lines both in front, across and wrapping around the entire block just to get into the store and buy something. It was insane and I can't forget that image to this day.

During one of her trips, my mom somehow managed to get into the presentation of an Indian fashion designer that was engaged in the import/export trade business with the Soviet Union. I recall how excited I was that she had bought me a two-piece outfit. It had a very intricate design and was cream colored. The fabric consisted of a very fine cotton. It was so fine and sheer that it almost looked transparent. On top were these big white flowers that consisted of a delicate and intricate pattern.

This was the mid-eighties, and what was in style was all the pleats, the shoulder pads, the snaps; and the details on the clothing were unlike anything I had seen before. The two-piece outfit I got to wear was actually one of the first creations of that Indian designer. The great thing it was aligned perfectly with my bold fashionista ways. It had the cool vibe I was aiming for. So, what happened next? Next thing I know somebody on the street laughed in my face and pointed at me saying that I was wearing a pajama.

I thought "alright I can handle being ridiculed for wearing this amazing cotton creation". Then, came a discovery about the fabric that was both perplexing and a surprise, let's say more of a disappointment in the quality of the fabric. Each time I would wear the outfit, the armpit area would turn blue whenever I would sweat. I tried everything to get

the discoloration out and nothing worked. My outfit was ruined.
Then I came to the US and bought a Calvin Klein T-shirt and when I looked at the label, I saw that it was made in India. Same issue again. Here I am thinking to myself what is up with Indian cotton? I made one more attempt and purchased an expensive Jean Paul Gaultier one of a kind designed shirt. It was so impressive that people stopped me on the streets and asked to take a picture with me. Same story though, made in India and blue armpits. So, now I'm thinking is it just my DNA and Indian cotton that just don't bind well together? I was tempted to go around asking people if they had the same issue with Indian cotton.

Finally, years later, I think I figured it out after studying textile chemical engineering. The change of color had something to do with the chemicals that were poured on the cotton during the processing stage as well as possibly pesticides that might have been used in the cotton fields. Everything is a molecule and every single molecule can have a chemical reaction. With that not every chemical is compatible with your body type. And, reactions like that can occur. The process involved in producing a textile consists of a series of physical processes and chemical reactions. Some reactions are more aggressive and harsher.

Additionally, the stats around about cotton are pretty staggering and delivering a huge blow to our Earth with each passing day. Did you know that "Every day we are trying to be conscious of our water consumption. We take shorter showers, close the tap when brushing our teeth etc. But what do we all have in our houses that consumes a 900 days' worth of drinking water? That will be your favorite cotton T-Shirt. And that's a lot of water; 2,700

liters to be exact. It may be a shock to you, right?
The fashion industry is a massive consumer and polluter of our fresh water. And one of the biggest culprits is cotton."

In the end, my love for cotton was completely crushed and I knew there had to be a better option out there for myself and the world. Labeling it organic still does not make it an acceptable fabric as the plant is not friendly to our ecosystem and cannot be sustained long-term. This the result of my observations which date back to when I traveled to Central Asia and visited the cotton fields, I had to read the disturbing accounts of field workers who burned themselves in the field, and even gave birth in the field. Just think of the atrocity of a woman being that pregnant and having to work? Grievous human rights violations are being perpetrated. That has kept me up at night and I know there is an urgency to finding a solution where everyone wins: consumers, workers and Mother Earth.

A second most widely purchased fabric is polyester. Maybe you are thinking this might be a possible alternative as it has been promoted as a great alternative to cotton. Another winning aspect for the consumer is that it is affordable and easier to care of (does not wrinkle as much as cotton).
When you take a close look at the yarn detail of the outfit you are wearing, most likely you will note that it is made of primarily polyester. Statistics show that the majority of world's clothing is made from polyester.
Almost every piece of clothing we buy is made with some polyester, the data shows. Although the data set is made up of mostly fast fashion

2. FABRICS: LONG-LASTING AND PLEASURABLE

retailers, it's not just fast fashion that loves polyester.
Lululemon joggers? Polyester, nylon and elastane. Gucci skirt? Polyester. And consumers are avidly purchasing them.

This synthetic fiber is derived predominantly from petroleum. Record rates have been set in the 21st century for polyester as it has overtaken cotton as the main textile fiber, ending hundreds of years of cotton's dominance. The global market for polyester yarn is expected to grow from $106 billion in 2022 to $174.7 billion by 2032. Yearly polyester fiber production is projected to exceed 92 million tons in the next 10 years – an increase of 47%.

However, not all polyester is produced from petroleum; it can also be made from natural polymers, like bioplastics, but those alternatives only make up a small fraction of polyester in the fashion industry.
The reason the industry loves polyester: it's hardy and versatile, used to create everything from athletic clothes to faux fur jackets to silky dresses. It is being marketed as more sustainable than some natural fibers due to the fact the production process doesn't require as much water or land as growing natural fibers like cotton.

Up to this point, polyester seems a great viable option and feels like a winner. Unfortunately, it is not as squeaky clean as it might sound. Research has shown that "The environmental effects of polyester's dominance over the clothing industry are varied.
For one, polyester requires a large amount of energy to produce. In 2015, polyester production for clothing emitted 282 billion tons of carbon dioxide, triple that of cotton. Furthermore, synthetic textiles

like polyester shed tiny pieces of plastic with every wash and wear. These plastic particles, called microplastics, pollute the oceans, freshwater and land and pose a danger to the animals that consume them, inhibiting their growth and reproduction. Scientists in Australia estimate that between 9.25 to 15.86 million tons of microplastics can be found on the ocean floor... A study in England found that marine mussels exposed to microplastics had broken DNA and deformed gills and digestive tubes." Microplastc pieces can be absorbed through the skin and inside the body wreak havoc on hormones, because it mimics estrogen and be dangerous for pre as well as post menopausal women.

And right now, even if the garment is made of cotton, linen, silk, the lining is still polyester. Even though polyester is considered durable, it's not very breathable. Our skin is not meant to be trapped inside polyester clothing for the day, accumulating heat and sweat.

Synthetic fibers are heat sensitive (have you not noticed labels stating you should keep these items away from flames?), so, when your body heats up, chemicals are inevitably released. They're reabsorbed into your skin, which can cause skin irritation. Additionally, synthetic fibers are not able to absorb the germs found in sweat, so your polyester clothes are a veritable breeding ground for bacteria. As our body's largest organ, how we treat our skin matters. With all of these potential risks to our health, this is where my biggest challenge as a designer comes into the picture.

Just when it seems we might have run out of options, there is a light at the end of the tunnel. I will explain next.

2. FABRICS: LONG-LASTING AND PLEASURABLE

LUXURIOUS, SUSTAINABLE AND ECO-FRIENDLY ALTERNATIVES

When you search the web these days, you might feel overwhelmed by the amount of information and suggestions for sustainable fabrics. If it is going to be a winning formula for both the people and the planet, then not only does fashion need to be sustainable, it will also have to fill the criteria of luxury as well as eco-friendliness.

The truth of the matter is that sustainable fashion "is a combination of many different fluid facets which include ethical business practices, supply chain transparency, minimal impact policies, give-back programs, and, arguably most important of all, the sustainable materials that make up our ethical wardrobe. On the positive side, environmentally friendly fabrics are becoming easier to find — if you know where to look. And the brands that use them are staking their claim for a better fashion future."

As a designer, I have made a conscious effort when producing all of my ready-to-wear collections to research each factory that I source from.

The new way of mindful luxury utilizes fabrics/materials that can be fast growing, native to the countries it grows in (meaning it justly supports their economic system), renews easily, it is long-lasting/durable and sustainable (good for the environment).

I have been studying and experimenting with another similar natural, plant-based fabric like cotton and it is bamboo. In my search, I knew it had to hold up to the quality standard and comfort provided by cotton in order to be a winner for the consumer, designer/manufacturer and the planet. Let's start to look into great options of the more **sustainable, luxurious fabrics** out there being used to change the game which I have personally vetted with my DoviArt Fashion line:

ORGANIC BAMBOO

Organic bamboo fabric will be showcased in my new summer collection that will debut next year. Some of the comments I have heard, from people who own clothing made from bamboo fabric and feedback I have received from my clients who I gave samples to, are saying that they loved it. They stated that it made them feel like they were almost wearing silk and that durability wise it was really good. Additionally, they mentioned that the comfort of it was comparable to wearing cotton. This is good news, because when you replace a fabric that has a long life with something which is comparable, but then it has a short life that would not make any sense and would be a recipe for failure.

The other thing to keep in mind is the process of producing fabric which is a dirty one with a lot of polluting ramifications. So, if you have to produce more and more of it to replace the one that you are trying to eliminate, because it wears out easily or loses its shape, then you might as well not bother replacing it. The key is finding a solution that addresses all of these issues.

2. FABRICS: LONG-LASTING AND PLEASURABLE

Organic bamboo seems to be that game changer as a plant-based alternative.

Research is showing that "When bamboo is harvested, it can be done without killing the plant itself. That means that bamboo can renew super quickly (it's one of the fastest growing plants on the planet). Like hemp, bamboo consumes more CO_2 than some trees. It doesn't require a lot of inputs and can survive on rainfall alone.

Organic bamboo can be turned into one of the most sustainable fabrics — but that doesn't mean it always is. Depending on how its processed, it could involve chemically intensive processes — and all the harmful impacts that come with it." That is where you, the consumer, have the right to inquire and find out exactly how it has been processed.

"Mechanically processed bamboo is a better-for-Earth way to wear bamboo (but sadly it makes up just a tiny amount of what we find on the market).

Look for organic bamboo fabric in raw form as opposed to that which is plasticized into bamboo rayon/viscose (…it's important to know the distinction, given most bamboo fabrics on the market are viscose/rayon)."

BAMBOO LYOCELL

This second type of bamboo is the one you should avoid. Despite claims out there that it is good for you, ethically sourced and eco-friendly fabric.

After investigating and studying the process of creating bamboo lyocell, I found from my research that it is "…like regular or TENCEL™ lyocell, and is also made in a closed-loop process that reuses chemicals and water.
However, bamboo can also be very unsustainable and it's easy to mistake closed-loop bamboo lyocell with bamboo viscose. Both of these require a whole host of chemicals to plasticize the pulp into silky fibers. So, look out for closed-loop bamboo lyocell, that is also processed with minimal toxic chemicals. A few brands making bamboo pajamas and bamboo socks, and the supplier Monocel for example, have started creating their own sustainable bamboo lyocell metrics. Either way, it's important to do a double take at transparency and other types of third-party certifications."

Moving on to the next option out there for you to consider, maybe not one of the best, but one worth considering.

2. FABRICS: LONG-LASTING AND PLEASURABLE

ORGANIC LINEN:

Linen is a very special fabric because it has the ability to cool your body. It has two great qualities: super light and breathable.

It has been shown to be very popular in many countries where the climate is hot especially during the summer months.

Linen is almost identical to hemp in terms of sustainability. The main difference with linen is that it is derived from the flax plant.
The growth of linen requires very little fertilizer, pesticide, and irrigation. Unlike hemp, linen is not as high-yielding. Linen's general popularity and reliability has made it a favorite fabric in everything from linen clothing to linen sheets.

The downside of the linen fabric: it wrinkles too easily. The fiber itself is not fine as cotton. And so, despite its popularity in some countries, its overall use has been rather limited in the fashion industry. Other than that, it is an excellent option as it has a luxurious feel to it and nothing compares to wearing it on a hot summer day.

Coming up we are going to explore animal derived natural fabrics which can be sustainable depending on the source.

SILK

Wearing silk is an unforgettable and super luxurious experience. At least, I found that to be true in my experience. There has been a bit of worship of silk in my family when it comes to silk.

A bias for silk you might say. Back in the sixties and seventies, the Soviet Union had a good relationship with China.

Silk import as a result was inevitable.

As young child, I remember my grandmother, who was a fashionista introducing me to silk when she would take me to her appointments with her seamstress for fittings.

For me, that planted the seed and I can say that is one of the reasons I am a designer today.

Thinking back to that special time with my grandmother, one funny story pops up in my head.

There was a jacquard fabric which had a bright purple violet background with silver hues. Jacquard fabric is textured fabric that has complex patterns woven into it, rather than printed, dyed, or embroidered on top.

It was so intricately weaved with these beautiful sliver flowers and it had this mesmerizing effect.

My grandmother ended up having a dress made out of this lush silk jacquard fabric and then she got another one with the red flowers. My wheels started turning in my head and I thought what if I cut a piece of that fabric and used it to make a dress for my favorite doll. I was probably five years old.

2. FABRICS: LONG-LASTING AND PLEASURABLE

It ended up becoming a kimono dress for my doll.
No one noticed that a piece had been cut out of it until my grandpa took the fabric to her seamstress to have the dress made and, of course, all they saw was this huge gaping hole in the middle.
They never let me forget that incident.
The disastrous experience made me shy away for the longest time from luxurious fabrics especially silk.

Years later when I was in school studying textile chemical engineering, I remember my professor re-igniting my interest in silk. I started to appreciate again the luxuriousness of silk.
The sound, that silk makes when you crinkle it, is unforgettable: similar to when you walk on cold, fresh, crisp snow.
The one thing to be aware of when purchasing silk is that there is also synthetic silk which looks from the outside almost like natural silk and it should not be confused with the real deal.
Easiest way to test it is by grabbing the silk and crinkling it by your ear. And, if you hear that fresh snow sound, then you know that it is authentic silk.

Additionally, silk has healing properties as it soothes your nerves. The most luxurious bed sheets and bed gowns are made of silk. There is good a reason for that because it helps you to have a better night's sleep.
Recently, it was noted that silk has another benefit: it has antibacterial properties which makes it great for your skin.
One fact to keep in mind is that it's not as absorbent to bodily fluids and it usually changes color when you sweat.

If that bothers you then it might not be for you, however, other than that small issue nothing compares to that sleek feeling.

Since silk is animal based, it does not burden the land. Silk originates from silkworms and they eat only mulberry leaves which essentially grow on a tree. A mulberry tree produces enough leaves to feed these worms. Silk is also known for it complete compostability making it great for the planet.

Silk is produced by either 'wild silkworms,' or, in most cases, domesticated silkworms. In principle, the production of silk should not harm the worms, but it has been shown that they end up dying when the silk is processed.
The fiber is derived when they break the cocoon of the silkworm to extract the worm out. If nature had its way the worms would break free on their own as they grow and develop.
Ultimately, with time they would transform into these magnificent butterflies.

This method might feel like an inhumane process for some of you. However, it doesn't stop here as the next step in getting those precious fibers is by boiling the worms. I felt overwhelmed by emotions when I learned this fact. Those worms are sacrificed in order to get us the silk fabric.

Looking on the bright side, there has been a recent discovery by a brilliant Israeli woman who is both an artist and a scientist on a way to save the worm.

2. FABRICS: LONG-LASTING AND PLEASURABLE

Neri Oxman, an MIT professor, has invented a robotic machine that unwraps the cocoon so it saves the worm, but sadly there still remains the fact that it will never develop into its fullest potential of a beautiful butterfly.

It seems there is more research being done on this hack and we will be seeing improvements on Neri Oxman's method in the years to come.

Moreover, some brands have started experimenting with silk made of yeast, sugar, and water. Until then, if you're looking for sustainable silk, peace silk might be a great alternative. Another disappointing fact is that the practices of sericulture (aka the silk industry) has been linked to slave labor.

Peace silk uses a humane type of sericulture and verifies its production under the World Fair Trade Organization Guarantee system.

Also known as 'Ahisma Silk' the nonviolent production process allows the silkworm to live a natural and humane life and eventually evolve into a butterfly.

The silkworms are bred under natural conditions (with no fungicides, sprays, or insecticides).

They're able to emerge on their own and carry on with their lives after the silk is collected. In contrast to most silk harvesting that requires the silkworms to be killed in their cocoon stage. You read right — no living creatures were inhumanely tortured and sacrificed in this type of silk fabric production!

As you read this, there will be some of you that will remain pro silk and some who might vow to never buy it again.

At least, now you are equipped with the knowledge of what it takes to make silk, and it will require your investigating further to see where the silk is coming from (who is the manufacturer, where was it sourced from etc.).

From there, you are now ready to make the decision of whether or not to buy it.

Again, I can't say it enough: knowledge is power and you have the power to move that needle, creating a lasting impact on the future of fashion by the choices you make starting today.

WOOL

Wool is another fabric that is expensive and luxurious for the same reason, because it's animal based that means it's the closest thing to our skin which makes us feel our best.

It gives us such a soft and cozy feeling. Interestingly enough you can actually make shirts out of wool especially when wool and silk are blended together, it provides superb quality and creates a luxurious experience for the consumer.

Wool can run on the expensive side because of the process and the limited quantity of sheep that are raised. Furthermore, it is time consuming to produce wool and requires a lot of labor. Therefore, the higher cost factor.

2. FABRICS: LONG-LASTING AND PLEASURABLE

The benefit of wool is that it does not take as many resources as, say, plant-based fabrics and the turnaround time is much shorter while the growth of the plant cycle can be extremely slow.
Our hair and nails grow faster than the plants, so you can imagine the length time needed to invest in a plant-based fabric.

Wool is considered a natural fiber and is also an alternative to plastic/petroleum-based synthetics like nylon and polyester.

The durability is great as it is long-lasting, and a bonus is that it does not require a lot of chemicals during the processing stage.

Furthermore, the process of extracting wool is done in a humane way. The sheep are not being tortured and for those of us who are animal lovers that is a plus.
Actually, it would probably be more torture for the sheep to carry all that wool during the warmer summer months.

Also, you can't beat the cuteness of sheep (that is if you have a soft spot for animals like I do).

Wool fabrics can biodegrade naturally. The fats on the wool can be broken down naturally with a solution made of the ashes. There is a way to decompose it naturally and that will inevitably make the fabric more expensive.

Buying expensive is not necessarily a negative, it is just about a mindset shift in your buying habits: making a conscious decision to invest in higher quality clothing that will last you for many years (sometimes a lifetime) versus buying numerous disposable outfits that add up over time and end up costing just as much as the higher quality, luxurious ones.

Wool is probably the most ecologically friendly fabric. There are also different types of wool out there. Some people don't like wool, especially that coarser type of wool, which has actually caused allergic reactions on sensitive skins such as rashes, itchiness etc.

Selecting a softer and higher quality type of wool will solve that problem as the feel of it is comparable to that of silk and will probably not create allergic reactions.

Then, there are several different varieties of animals from which wool is derived but probably not worn as much, such as llamas, alpacas and camel. For instance, camel wool is used mainly to make blankets (used to make sweaters as well) that provide a lot of warmth for harsher winter climates.

These can be researched further, and you can find the one that is the best fit for you.

As you have been reading through this chapter, I hope you have gained some valuable insights that you can start applying right away to the way you shop from this point on.
You now have acquired the knowledge you need to pick out the most sustainable fabric options.

2. FABRICS: LONG-LASTING AND PLEASURABLE

Change begins with you, and you can vote with your wallet!

You have only barely scratched the surface in your continued journey in learning more about the inner workings of the fashion industry.

The fall of this glamorous industry is inevitable if it continues at the rate it has (sadly enough it has already begun) and yet, there is a glorious victory awaiting if we all collectively come together as part of the solution. Don't you want to say: "yes, I was part of the legacy that changed the trajectory of the future of fashion"?

This is a huge opportunity for the fashion industry to create a new revolutionary system fueled by all the parties involved whether you are a consumer, a designer or manufacturer/supplier.

As you become more aware of the underlying issues in the textile production end of things, you can start to challenge the status quo, demand answers and apply pressure for change.
This will be an opportunity for the textile production industry to wake up and take notice.

Suppliers and apparel producers will be more open to demonstrate to the world that they are able to fulfill the new requirements and can be profitable as well.

When you buy, you should understand and know all the aspects involved in creating that outfit you are wearing, including the production aspect of it.

The textile production industry has been operating with the fact that consumers have had no interest in how they conduct business, so why not keep doing things the way they have for centuries despite the ramifications it will have on future generations.

If you are a mother, father, grandparent you should be anxiously concerned with the future of your family and the heavy toll that the lack of care the textile production sector is placing on all of us.
The time is now to hold them accountable.
How can you do that? Stay tuned as we will be discussing the textile production process next.

KEY POINTS

- Choosing low quality fabrics results in unsustainable fashion.
- A majority of the materials that are used to make our clothes cause harm to humans and animals. Sometimes even both. Long-term damaging chemicals and microplastics are released into our environment which should be a cause of alarm for the future of our well-being and the planet.
- In order for sustainable fashion to be a winner for both the people and the planet, it will also have to fill the criteria of luxury as well as eco-friendliness.
- Whether you are a consumer or designer, you can improve the conditions of the world by choosing sustainable clothing. There are some great fabric options to choose from. You have the power to investigate and decide which sources you are going to support with your money.
- You are an integral part of the new glamorous, luxurious fashion revolution. You are the solution to the fashion industry woes!

What is your favorite fabric? Why?

When buying clothes do you check the label to find out what material it is made from?

Do you still think you cannot afford clothes made from high quality natural fabrics?

3

Chapter 3

TEXTILE PRODUCTION REIMAGINED

3. TEXTILE PRODUCTION REIMAGINED

The fashion industry is at a tipping point and has to make a choice on how it will deal with excessive water usage, dangerous chemicals, carbon emissions as well as massive amounts of waste. The elegant image that you might have about the fashion industry is one they would like you to believe; however, it is actually a mirage. The truth of the matter is that when you delve deeper into their business practices, you then can see how unglamorous and shameful it is.

Moreover, retailers and designers have a responsibility with not only where they are sourcing their materials from, but also with giving a safe working place to the people making clothes for them. Responsible sourcing by major global brands like Gap, Zara, H&M are vital to improving the industry.

Unfortunately, the factories they use frequently lack basic safety features like emergency exits, enough staircases, and up-to-date electrical systems. "Managers of these factories have proven willing to sacrifice lives by ordering workers to remain in structurally unsound buildings."

Research studies have noted that the fashion industry has been an engine for global development. One of the world's largest consumer industries: — generating $1.5 trillion in annual apparel and footwear revenues in 2016 — employing around 60 million people along its value chain. This shows how much power it has to make scalable transformative changes. Should the consumer demand these reforms, then this change can happen at a much faster speed than the pace it is going at right now.

These research data show us that this is also a big chance for designers, manufacturers and retailers to do their part by adopting as well as committing to new higher conscious business practices that will set the foundation for generations to come. Even though it might feel like a daunting task as to how the industry will seize the opportunity to reverse the course and positively impact the planet as well as provide quality to its consumers, there has been an emergence of hope as various creative and innovative entrepreneurs have begun initiating change.

For instance, in calling my own luxury design practice into account, I have made the commitment to make my own patterns and locally produce them in the US. Only the highest quality materials are used that are both eco-friendly and great for the health of customers as well as fitting their requirements. Also, I train my hand-picked design team and make sure they are aligned with my vision of sustainability, providing exceptional luxury quality for my customers and committing to the DoviArt best practices. I have made it a criterium that when I hire, I only work with talents possessing superior design and tech skills. Even then, I still invest time and effort to train each one of them so they can replicate my way and standards for designing. I do not allow for compromises for the sake of profitability and targeted sales goals. All of my designs are handcrafted meticulously and I am involved in every step of the process from the making of it all the way down to the technical elements. Plus, every design creation is individually customized for my clients.

3. TEXTILE PRODUCTION REIMAGINED

Right now, the DoviArt line sells only online and in my boutique. There is no excess surplus inventory — no losses incurred.

I do not produce if it does not sell and therefore that means I am not sitting on a surplus of inventory. Technology is absolutely amazing as I currently work with an app that scans your body and custom fits the design to your figure details.

The majority of my clients are global, and the clothes are created through virtual instructions based on the app. There is nothing more satisfying for a designer than making a client happy. Providing unique custom-made designs with the person you are working with in mind is what it is all about.

I am sure there are a lot of you who would love to have your essence captured in the outfits you are wearing and that is what DoviArt strives to provide — an unparalleled one-of-a-kind luxurious fashion and shopping experience.

Some of the major department stores and retailers could follow suit by just starting to offer less inventory, and that way maybe consumers can begin to get used to the idea of there being less out there. I think that could be one starting point. Yet, we need a lot more movers and shakers out there in the textile production innovation world.

For a long time, I wondered if there were any change agents in the world of fashion industry. Then, I learned of some remarkable individuals pioneering great initiatives. Let's take a peek into a few of these remarkable individuals.

TEXTILE PRODUCTION INNOVATORS

One such inspiring individual is Stephanie Benedetto who is creating ripples of change in the textile industry and the world, while urging others to have courage in their convictions and act on their beliefs.

Stephanie is the descendant of an Austrian immigrant who arrived at the Lower East Side of New York and was chasing the 'American Dream'. There he started a business, one that generated profit while doing good for the planet. His mission was to repurpose old fabrics and furs brought over by other immigrants which he transformed into beautiful fashion garments.

"One hundred years later, this profitable clothing business with humble beginnings would inspire the Austrian Immigrant's great-granddaughter, Stephanie Benedetto, to leave her job as a corporate attorney and become a fashion tech and sustainability entrepreneur. Stephanie returned to her roots and sparked disruption with the goal of building a business to change the world, scaling her grandfather's efforts for even greater impact.

Stephanie is the CEO and Founder of Queen of Raw. She is a visionary entrepreneur, creating opportunity out of the seemingly insurmountable challenges facing the fashion industry. Today, $120 billion worth of excess fabric sits in warehouses and 87% of fiber input used for clothing ends up burned or in landfills. Benedetto wanted to eliminate the excess water, waste, and emissions that had become an

3. TEXTILE PRODUCTION REIMAGINED

inherent part of the value chain for clothing production. She sought to turn pollution into profit through the creation of a global marketplace that allowed users to list, sell, and buy deadstock fabric. This led to Queen of Raw, which offers new life to sustainable materials, including organic cotton, peace silk, faux leather and fur, and quality luxury deadstock fabrics."

She is using technology to scale impact. Queen of Raw has figured out a revolutionary way to use a supply chain software powered by artificial intelligence that is "altering the linear economic model typical of the fashion industry and transforms it into a circular economic model, protecting the environment while driving value financially."
It is creatively using technology to serve the betterment of the world by driving sustainability at scale, repurposing textile waste, so it can be turned into something beautiful."

Benedetto states that "A marketplace to sell waste is great; it's powerful, but it's kind of just slapping a band aid on the problem."

That leaves the root of the problem to solve. How do you go about minimizing waste? She goes on further and says, "That's where we leverage our incredible partnership with SAP, the world's leading provider of business software that helps companies run better as well as supports the capturing of data through machine learning, AI, and blockchain so they can act on the waste (and water) challenge at hand," said Benedetto. Since it was founded in 2018, "Queen of Raw has already saved 1 billion gallons of water".

Now, that should give everyone hope and I was truly blown away by the creative genius out there that can support the industry to move from the mode of crisis to victory. Queen of Raw gives us that promising potential (in this case technology which we are inundated with and could be utilized for a higher purpose) that can reimagine fashion, textiles, and value chains.

Innovative and creative solutions like Queen of Raw are but just tip of the iceberg. Another pioneer setting new standards and spearheading the reshaping of the textile production industry is the notable Mary Ruppert-Stroescu, an associate professor of fashion design who has patented a new process for recycling cotton fabric. Ruppert-Stroescu's RECLEM system transforms the way garments are designed, manufactured and recycled. With RECLEM, she provides a "roadmap for how designers and manufacturers can deconstruct and reuse discarded textile products, and add further value by reassembling — or 'upcycling' — them into something fresh and new."

Ruppert-Stroescu notes that roughly 15% of cloth intended for apparel winds up as scrap on the cutting room floor. And though an estimated 95% of retail clothing is recyclable, the vast majority ends up in landfills — more than 20 billion pounds annually in the United States alone.

3. TEXTILE PRODUCTION REIMAGINED

She goes on to describe the RECLEM process:

"The first step is to collect fabric and slice it into strips, squares or other small pieces. Though synthetic fabrics, such as nylon, can be melted down and spun into new thread, re-spinning cotton or other natural fabrics is difficult and results in shorter fibers. Our goal is to maintain as much structural integrity as possible. Once cut, the fabric pieces are laid — either by hand or via digital plotter — into a surface design within the garment pattern shape on thin, biodegradable film. This holds the design in place while pieces are stitched together. When the fabric is washed, the film dissolves and the sections are ready to assemble.

There are crafters who stitch over film, and there are bespoke designers who cut up T-shirts and knit with them," Ruppert-Stroescu said. "What's unique here is the full sequence. There is no other process for breaking down a textile while maintaining its integrity; designing a new piece within the pattern; stitching it together; dissolving it; and then sewing the finished garment."

Ruppert-Stroescu's process involves shaping fabric, rather than cutting it, grain can be customized, and patterns can easily be scaled up or down.
"RECLEM pushes designers to engineer the straight-of-grain, details and color into the shape of the product itself, rethinking both the design and manufacturing process," she said. "The material utilization is 100%."

In addition, the RECLEM system largely maps onto existing commercial machinery and could be seamlessly integrated into large-scale production, Ruppert-Stroescu says.

Furthermore, she notes that, compared to creating new cloth, RECLEM dramatically lowers material costs while resulting in no loss of tensile strength, wrinkle recovery, water repellency or abrasion resistance.

Consumers are also a critical part of the process as, with increased transparency, there is a need to educate them as to the scope of textile waste. She goes on to mention that "Brands serve their customers. Companies will put resources into sustainability when consumer attention to true Earth-preserving practices makes walking that walk a real competitive advantage."

So, again, point being made, you the consumer are such an integral part of this process and as you investigate the truth, you can then make more demands which will inevitably force them to change their business practices for the better.

Another promising initiative was the International Detox Campaign which was based on the Greenpeace studies that "showed that more than two-thirds of all branded apparel tested and sold worldwide contains hazardous pollutants, including the products of large fashion manufacturers and retailers such as Calvin Klein, Levi's, Zara and Marks & Spencer. Greenpeace tested 233 garments from 37 different brands, which were produced in 19 different countries and sold in 29 different countries.

3. TEXTILE PRODUCTION REIMAGINED

The Detox campaign has continued to encourage global fashion brands to detoxify their products and supply chains by making transparent all pollutants still used in the manufacturing process and to completely eliminate them.

A further move to shake up the fashion industry is being organized by Akshay Sethi, the cofounder and CEO of Ambercycle, and he is doing this with a new textile recycling process (Ambercycle is a science R&D company that is making climate positive plastics). His unique technology produces virgin-grade polymers from textile waste. Then, this polymer is converted into yarn, and this yarn is made into apparel, eliminating the need for new fossil-based materials. He recently acquired a $21 million round of funding to continue to scale Ambercycle's work, which includes a recent collaboration with H&M.

WAYS TO MOVE FORWARD AND RECOMMENDATIONS

To lead us into the 21st century, here are a few recommendations by the European Parliament which could also be blueprint for all other countries to follow, including the US, in order to move us away from conventional methods into new modes of operation and learnings.

Increasing the longevity of fashion through:

- **Slow fashion.** The industry needs to convince consumers to buy fewer clothes of better quality and to keep them for longer. The philosophy includes reliance on trusted supply chains, small-scale production, traditional crafting techniques, using local materials and trans-seasonal garments. It calls for a change in the economic model, towards selling fewer clothes.

- **Fashion as a service.** New business models could increase the number of wears of particular items by using the principles of the sharing economy. Some brands already offer clothes as a service – leasing their clothes instead of selling them – taking their example from already well-established services of renting wedding and special occasion wear, protective clothes and newer services of renting maternity and baby clothes.

- **Improved collection for re-use and up-cycling.** Encourage and support brands that are taking pioneering steps by selling their used clothes in their regular shops to make buying second-hand clothes easier and offering up-cycling or instructions for up-cycling.

- **Smart and instant fashion.** Smart fashion could bring clothes of the future that may use smart technology to instantly adjust to the wishes of the consumer, by changing colors for example, which would also reduce the need to produce multiple versions of the same garment. Instant fashion could enable on-demand production at point of sale.

3. TEXTILE PRODUCTION REIMAGINED

Consumers would be able to get what they want produced locally with no overproduction. Some smaller brands are already avoiding overproduction by producing only what consumers order.

Improved collection and recycling through:

- **Circular fashion.** Like the circular economy in general, circular fashion seeks to reduce waste to a minimum and keep the materials within the consumption and production loop as long as possible. When clothes are no longer used, they should be either sold as second-hand clothes or recycled, as seen with the RECLEM process.

- **Extended producer responsibility (EPR) and in-store collection.** Producers and importers can be made legally responsible for ensuring that used clothes are reused or recycled, with companies either organizing their own programs or contributing financially to an accredited collectively responsible organization.

Targeting consumers and the role they play in the process:

- **Raising consumer awareness.** Through campaigns or providing information on sustainability in stores, or through tags on clothes, it may be possible to educate consumers to buy only what they need and to choose more sustainable options. Research shows that consumers are generally in favor of environmentally responsible fashion, but that this is not necessarily reflected in their actual behavior. A number of factors drive consumers away from sustainable fashion, including higher prices (although the number of environmentally conscious consumers who are ready to pay more for the sustainable option is on the rise) and the notion that recycled clothes may be of a lower quality and that they are produced in less polished styles, etc.

- **Increased transparency and environmental labeling.** Some companies already provide consumers with information on the environmental footprint of their products, such as CO_2 emissions or water use. Choosing a more sustainable option could be made easier through clear and standardized labeling of environmentally friendly products.

- **Better washing and drying instructions.** As washing and drying make a large contribution to the environmental impact of clothes, the industry could help by providing consumers with better information on how to reduce this impact, for instance, on care labels. Others offer step-by-step repair and care guidelines on their websites.

The fashion industry now has numerous approaches it can start to implement and has a clear opportunity to act differently. There are methods provided that can continue to allow it to pursue profit and growth while simultaneously creating new value for society and therefore for the world economy. It comes with an urgent need to place environmental, social, and ethical improvements at the forefront of the textile industry and on management's agenda. From my experience I have seen that when you have the best interest

3. TEXTILE PRODUCTION REIMAGINED

of those you service with your product and brand, profits and growth come exponentially on their own with much less effort than you think. Humanity wants to rally around a winning formula for all and support businesses that are doing things for the well-being of society and the Earth rather than what is propelled by only greed and profit. Those days are coming to a rapid close.

Research projections are providing evidence that fashion brands' profitability levels are at risk in the range of at least 3 percentage points if they don't act determinedly, and soon. This is evidence that there is a clear need to act differently.
The good news is that by changing practices, the industry can both stop the negative impact and generate a high amount of value for society, while also protecting profitability. It is estimated that the world economy would gain about $171.5 billion annually if the fashion industry would successfully address those environmental and social issues.

Akshay Sethi states "You can't force sustainability; it has to be a desire". This applies to all of us from the consumer all the way to the supplier as well as all the middlemen involved. So, what role will you have in this collective shift towards a new, slow and luxurious way of fashion? Every drop can eventually become that expansive, bountiful ocean where everyone is thriving including our planet.

However, we need to still keep in mind that there is a call for more trailblazers and pioneers in galvanizing the speed in the process of change. I have hope for our fashion industry to turn itself around and become the beacon/model for others to emulate.

Setting the trend is not easy, but it can be done when everyone is aboard, from the consumer to the designer, to the retailer, to the manufacturer, supplier etc. I know we can do it.

The question is: are you ready to be a part of the paradigm shift and step into this transformative world of slow fashion where quality and luxury are the requirements? I have faith it can be done with will and determination to make this world more of a sanctuary for now and future generations to come.

KEY POINTS

- There is a huge opportunity for designers, manufacturers and retailers to do their part by adopting as well as committing to new higher conscious business practices that will set the foundation for generations to come.

- Educating and being more transparent with the consumer is a critical component in creating long lasting changes in their habits, as well as perceptions of slow fashion vs. fast fashion (promoting higher quality and less expendable clothing).

- There needs to be a more significant push to improving collection and recycling in the textile industry (e.g. circular fashion).

- More and more we are witnessing up and coming pioneers in the creation of technology and processes that will support this new way of fashion and doing business.

Would you pay a little extra for the clothes made using more environmentally friendly process?

What do you do with clothes you don't want anymore?

Do you even care how your clothes are made?

Chapter 4
REINVENTING SHIPPING SOLUTIONS

4. REINVENTING SHIPPING SOLUTIONS

For the past two years, the pandemic has impacted the fashion logistics and its supply chain with long-lasting consequences. The numerous lockdowns we faced as a global community made it challenging for products to cross the frontiers and reach the final consumer.

The fashion industry is heavily dependent on contracts signed with companies based in countries that were at the epicenter of the virus at the beginning of the pandemic, such as China and Italy. Covid-19 had a negative impact on the textile industry in Asian countries, a significant number of which is constituted by raw material manufacturers for several other nations.

According to the Reuter's September 2021 report, fashion brands like Benetton are increasingly turning away from globe-spanning supply chains and low-cost manufacturing hubs in Asia, in a shift that could prove a lasting legacy of the COVID-19 pandemic. Italy's Benetton is bringing production closer to home, boosting manufacturing in Serbia, Croatia, Turkey, Tunisia and Egypt, with the aim of halving production in Asia by the end of 2022, in a statement released by Benetton's Chief Executive Massimo Renon. This has a significant impact on the livelihood and economy of Asian countries which ultimately puts the burden on an already overtaxed population, especially in the poorer Asian nations where slave labor is already a dire humanitarian issue. This shift in manufacturing is much easier to do in Europe or Middle East because of their historical tradition of exceptional skills in the art of sewing and knitting. Knowing how to sew and knit is a matter of pride in their culture.

However, this has also created a backlog for some countries as for instance, in my recent conversations with fashion designers in my home country of Lithuania, they have stated they have not been able to produce their collections on time, because of an increase in large scale Scandinavian orders that have taken precedence over their orders. In the US, unfortunately there is a lack of skilled workers. When I was researching where to produce my clothes locally this issue kept coming up — the lack of skilled workers trained in basics such as sewing and knitting.

In the report, Reuters goes on to state that **"a shipping container that used to cost $1,200-1,500 can cost $10,000-15,000, with no certainty of the delivery date."**
Additionally, the cancellation of orders affected a large number of micro and small retail companies. COVID-19 has also affected the season calendar.
As a result, reduced production forcedly encouraged slow fashion and the use of already manufactured products.
Then, there is also the environmental impact of international shipping which we will look at next.

4. REINVENTING SHIPPING SOLUTIONS

THE IMPACT OF CURRENT SHIPPING METHODS AND SOLUTIONS

Things can get complicated when it comes to the subject of international shipping and shopping sustainability. What requires a deeper reflection is that if we are purchasing ethical fashion from the other side of the world, then one could also assume any positive impact gained is nullified by a negative impact from carbon emissions. It is actually not that simple. Every action has a reaction, so which choice has the least negative impact?

That requires us to understand on a much deeper level the impact of our individual purchases and we need to consider the entire journey the piece of clothing has taken before it gets to us.

Chances are, no matter how sustainable a fashion brand might be, that item of clothing has, at some point and in some form, travelled around the world.

The journey is rather complex and lengthy. Rarely are raw materials grown, processed, sewn, and sold all in one location. Every stage of the supply chain has some form of impact on the environment.

When we take into account shipping specifically, the impact on the environment is considerable. Research has shown that "Ships handle roughly 90% of global trade, transporting nearly 10 billion metric tons (11 billion tons) of goods per year. It has been estimated that shipping accounts for 2.5% of the world's total CO_2 emissions and a 2015 report from the European Parliament estimated that number could rise as high as 17% by 2050."

With these dire stats, the issue of the current state of our shipping methods had me contemplating on the way I conduct business and how I would like to improve in this area. During a recent trip I made to Iceland for a fashion photo shoot, and after I started to review my latest project at the time (which was to produce a new ready-to-wear line that would be made available in Iceland), I had kind of mapped out a vision of what it would look like: order the fabric in South Korea, Japan or China (China looked like the more achievable option at the time, as with the other countries you needed some strong connections and partnerships).

Then, the fabric would be delivered to the factory in Peru where the manufacturing would take place. A much more realistic and cost-effective plan would have been to also source the fabric, such as wool and leather, in Peru as well as manufacture it there.

However, with silk I was thinking that would not be possible as Peru is not a producer of silk. Then, the product would be flown to Iceland as I had established a working relationship with boutiques in Iceland. All of this had me thinking about all of these countries and the transfer between them from South Korea/China to Peru to Iceland. What a mind-blowing amount of fuel was being used to transport my creations and how much waste was involved in the process!

My carbon footprints were weighing on my mind. The amount of greenhouse-gas emissions that fashion contributes to our climate woes is tremendous. When you start envisioning the trajectory of it all from start to finish, it is actually insanity what we are doing to our precious planet in the name of fashion. Additionally, one has to take into account the amount it takes to ship the clothes.

4. REINVENTING SHIPPING SOLUTIONS

For instance, in my case, it takes almost 40 days to ship from the time it leaves the factory in Korea or China to reach me wherever I am (Peru in this case), and then not to mention the extra time to transport it to the Iceland boutiques.

All of this contemplation and in-depth studying of the fashion logistics as well as the supply chain made me realize that for the DoviArt designs, and in my opinion for the future of the fashion, the best method is to localize everything as much as possible from sourcing the fabric to manufacturing to selling it in the country where you have set up your boutiques.

The future requires us to make fashion as local as we possibly can, if we are to save our planet and create more streamlined ROIs in a way that will also benefit factory worker in another part of the world.

Of course, there are still those who will continue to order online, but we can educate and encourage consumers to order from designers who are using local materials and manufacturers.

Again, I can't say it enough — the consumer also needs to do her/his part to become more savvy in asking "who designed my clothes and are they following a sustainable, locally produced garment?".

If designers are not yet at the point of localizing the majority of their operations, then, at the very least, they can still ship to other countries through alternative methods: for example one in which they are employing a fashion forward smooth and flexible freight solution.

This would be a step in the right direction by designers and fashion retailers acting responsibly towards the environment and striving to minimize the environmental impact of their products throughout their whole life-cycle.

For instance, fashion retailer Varner — one of Scandinavia's leading textile companies — is growing with increased production volumes and opening of new stores. To keep expanding but still remain close to the market, they needed a reliable and sustainable freight solution with high capacity. Following are a few insights into the "customized solution that Greencarrier Freight Services created for Varner, enabling a smooth and more sustainable transport of their fashion goods." The textile industry is now examining more closely shipping methods and setting new requirements which employ reliable and sustainable ways of transporting goods.

Fashion is constantly and rapidly changing. A company of Varner's size and growth needs to keep up with these changes to stay close to the market. And, they have to deliver products quickly and regularly to the stores. To manage further expansion, Varner needed a freight solution with high capacity. Varner has pegged itself as a value driven company that is always aiming to do responsible and sustainable business. In a statement, they indicated that "being a part of the textile industry means we have a responsibility towards the environment, and we strive to minimize the environmental impact of our products throughout their whole life-cycle. An important part of this is to transport the products in a more sustainable way."

4. REINVENTING SHIPPING SOLUTIONS

They have utilized intermodal transport by using the combination of road, sea and rail freight.
A freight solution carrier that has aligned well with the Varner vision of sustainability and the expansion in their business has been to sign a contract with Greencarrier Freight Services. Varner summarizes how their process works: "In short, our trailers are loaded with the goods in Istanbul and are driven to a port nearby.

We then put the trailers on a vessel shipping them to Trieste, Italy. Here, the trailers are unloaded and moved to railway wagons for transportation to Kiel, Germany. Another ferry carries the trailers to Gothenburg, Sweden. The last way to Varner's central warehouse in Vänersborg is done by road."

They have gone to claim that this way of transporting is a lot friendlier towards the environment: "By replacing main parts of the road transport to sea and rail freight, we are reducing CO_2 emission by almost 70%. So, even though the freight solution includes several steps, it is both more sustainable and efficient."

Even with their claim which seems like an alternative for now, I feel there is a lot more room for improvement to reduce the carbon footprint. I see a future where the combined shipping method will need to be elevated to the next level; we can do better than that! Unfortunately, we are not all at the capacity and size as Varner.
What about all the smaller to mid-size designers and textile companies out there?

The combination of shipping methods employed by Varner is one of the band-aid alternatives out there now for larger size retailers and couture designers, however, with the rising cost of fuel that we have witnessed due to anything from natural disasters to wars, we can't continue to ignore the exorbitant cost of shipping.

TIPS FOR WHAT CONSUMERS CAN DO NOW

1. Avoid fast shipping:

When you hit that expedited shipping button on your order, it means that your item will be delivered to you via plane instead of a cargo ship. Even though ships are not ideal ways, yet when the item is sent to you via plane, it results in significantly more carbon emissions than via ship.

2. Select in-store or centralized pick-up options:

Some vendors provide this alternative and using these types of delivery options will significantly reduce your personal carbon footprint as it will mean less courier/van transport — couriers can deliver bulk deliveries to these locations instead of having to go door-to-door. Collect your items via public transport, by bike, or on foot for bonus points.

3. Find ways to reduce overall consumption:

Think about going with a minimalist approach like adopting a capsule wardrobe, and only purchase items that you really need, that are high-quality, and will last you a long time. If you resonate with this option, try to find items from your local vintage boutique for secondhand clothing.

To keep up with these times and changing dynamics in shipping logistics brings me back to the aforementioned solution — what the future needs and is requiring us is to become local. We need to keep our designers of all levels in business, sustainable and doing good for every part of the eco-chain as well as the entire human race. And consumers can also be kept very satisfied with a higher quality of fashion but with less of it. As the saying goes: less is more. Quality vs. quantity. This a momentous time for all of us to move towards a more socially, economically and environmentally conscious alternative that will serve us for generations to come.

With that, let's explore some of the great benefits of locally sourcing which will ultimately solve the shipping and cost crisis in the long run.

BENEFITS OF LOCAL SOURCING AND PRODUCTION

Local sourcing and production is a two-pronged process that falls on the shoulders of both the designer and the consumer by the choices they make. Consumers when making their purchases have the option of choosing designers who are mindfully following this localized process and also advocating to purchase only from their own country's wealth of locally produced clothes.

Designers can make a conscious effort to source and oversee all aspects of their designs in the country of origin and to establish local hubs in the country of their choice such as China, Bangladesh, Vietnam and so on. They will need to have all hands on deck and be immersed in the entire process from start to finish. Investments of such kind will also have ripple effects on the country you decide to set up shop in and on the environment with a movement towards the enormous reduction in carbon dioxide emissions. Great aligned partnerships can be initiated at a fraction of the cost from the current mode we are in, where we are shipping from one end of the earth to the other before it reaches the consumer. And, yes, it will take work and building relationships, yet the benefits you will reap for years to come will be unprecedented.

To support local sourcing, the following research by Thomas, the industry's leading supplier discovery and product sourcing platform, makes a great case for it:

4. REINVENTING SHIPPING SOLUTIONS

"Consumer landscapes are continuing to change while businesses are adjusting for the new normal. Manufacturers and industrial companies across the world are working hard to maintain and strengthen their supply chains. And companies who preferred to source internationally to save on costs, are seeking other cost-effective solutions.

The growing reality is that procurement professionals actually prefer to source locally. Furthermore, in a survey conducted by Thomas, they mentioned that "nearly half of buyers (46.7 percent) actually 'rarely or never' prefer to source globally at all".

ADVANTAGES OF USING LOCAL SUPPLIERS

According to the Thomas research, listed below are several great reasons why buyers prefer to keep the supply chain as close to home as possible.

1. More Flexibility

You never know when an opportunity will strike or a challenge will arise. Buyers prefer knowing what the growth pattern is for the product they are sourcing before they actually choose a partner — and ability to scale is key. For instance, you can receive a highly lucrative bid from a great customer, or an existing client may need you to ramp up to meet demand. Will you be ready?

If you source locally, the answer will probably be yes. That's because local suppliers are typically more reactive than suppliers who are farther away. They can deliver products quicker, and it is much easier for a supplier to coordinate a shipment across the neighborhood than around the world.

2. Greater Control

The further away you are from elements of your supply chain, the less control you have over them. Suppliers may say that they treat all of their customers and purchase orders the same, but if they anticipate a site visit or a drop-in meeting from you, chances are they will keep you top of mind.

Face-to-face visits will allow you to address any concerns and ensure all products meet your standards. There's also less chance of things getting "lost in translation," which often occurs when working with big teams of people, many of whom aren't actually on the floor and touching your products.

Today, more manufacturers use videos of their factory to connect with more customers when travel is difficult or has restrictions.

3. Reduced Supply Chain Costs (Includes Shipping)

If you're tightening your budget, you should consider tightening your supply chain as well. The amount of money companies spend on logistics every year is staggering, with North American companies shelling out over $1 billion every year.

North American businesses send and receive parts and products all over the continent and the expenses can add up as quickly as the miles. Even then, these pieces have to be stored in warehouses until they are shipped again to the next supplier or, if you're lucky, the customer.

Many of these costs can be reduced by localizing your supply chain. And, with less money being sunk into logistics, there will be less weighing down your bottom line.

4. Good for The Community

It stands to reason that if sourcing locally increases your bottom line, it would do the same for other suppliers and manufacturers in your area, which can be a big boon to your local economy and the people who live there.

Happy, well-paid employees are more likely to invest in local businesses. Additionally, respected and well-off businesses are in a position to contribute to communities through fundraising, volunteering, benefits, and sponsored activities.

5. More Revenue

Local sourcing doesn't just help save money; it can also help you generate more of it. That's because companies in your region may be impressed by your efforts to keep a tight and fast-paced supply chain, which can help you attract new customers.

Integrate your commitment to local sourcing into your marketing and selling efforts. In fact, consider integrating it into your unique selling proposition.

6. It Helps the Environment

Localizing your supply chain represents a tremendous opportunity to help the environment. When you reduce shipping and storage, you also reduce emissions and energy usage. Sourcing locally not only contributes to green manufacturing, but ultimately helps you build consumer confidence. When consumers buy with confidence, the business benefits from increasing positive brand awareness and customer loyalty.

To give you some inspiration and hope for the future, I noted a rising fashion designer who is making quite an imprint and creating an impact in the call for more locally sourced higher fashion: Joseph Ribkoff's stylish, versatile creations and trend-setting designs have been leading the Canadian fashion scene for several years now by providing luxurious clothing for women with dynamic lifestyles who want to stand out from the crowd. Visionaries like Joseph Ribkoff are focusing

4. REINVENTING SHIPPING SOLUTIONS

on domestic production of clothing which is in alignment with Ethical Fashion and truly giving us hope for the future that local sourcing is possible. Joseph is showing us that it can be done — another great trailblazing pioneer in the new way of conducting fashion luxury with a high set of values, ethics and conscience.

Conscious consumers can easily use their wallets to vote companies and brands up or down based on their actions and levels of transparency throughout their business operations. My personal viewpoint is in alignment with the summarized research findings that "all participants in all parts of the value chain have a role to play in driving decarbonization and bringing about real and lasting change for the better in the fashion industry.

Given their potential to act as the main drivers of accelerated abatement, brands and retailers face a call to collaborate with others in the value chain to invest for long-term social and environmental benefits. Not only can they effect change in their own operations, but they can also support decarbonization efforts elsewhere in the industry and help consumers make more sustainable purchasing choices."

The future of fashion is bright and at the same time we have to keep in mind that there is no silver bullet, no quick fix scheme; rather, it will boil down to a combination of a lot of small innovations as well as a few radical changes. The change starts with us the designers leading all the way to the consumer. What will set us up collectively as winners is the willingness, ability and drive to be a change agent creating needle moving impact in the fashion world.

Whatever aspect we're touching in this book about sustainability and environmental protection is like a tangled yarn and a lot more complicated that we might have anticipated. Everything is connected in more than one way.

The companies that are claiming they are completely green or sustainable still have a lot of room for improvement and it might just be bandaid solutions for now. At the same time, some larger fashion brands might not even be fully transparent about their practices.

So, only time will tell as to the longevity and long-standing solutions that they are now offering in the name of sustainability. Same goes for the expectations the customers are putting on the clothing manufacturers and designers.

The main question here is "Is it even possible to be 100% sustainable or green? Can we do better?" Absolutely. "Is it going to be easy?" No. "Is it worth it?" Yes! And, our future depends on it.

KEY POINTS

- As innovative shipping solutions develop, for the time being using a freight solution that combines road, sea and rail freight has advantages that are a lot friendlier towards the environment in the reduction of CO_2 emissions.
- Keeping the supply chain as close to home as possible (local sourcing and production) is the way to go in order to improve cost and efficiency across the value chain for the better good of all.
- Local sourcing and production depend on connecting with the right partners. Find a partner(s) who is aligned with your vision in the countries you are looking to locally produce in.
- Social and environmental responsibility have risen higher on the list of factors influencing purchasing decisions.
- As a conscious consumer you have the ability to raise the standards of the brands by asking "is it sustainable, ethical and how is it being delivered — what shipping methods are being used? Is there a lower carbon footprint shipping method being used?".
- Designers and retail brands will be challenged to become more radical in how they behave in all aspects of fashion logistics in order to create a fashion forward future for the better good of all.

What are your thoughts on localized sourcing, manufacturing, shipping??

Do you ever consider shipping when purchasing something, not only cost, but environmental impact?

Do you personally think 100% green is possible?

5

Chapter 5
NEW STANDARDS IN COUTURE DESIGN

5. NEW STANDARDS IN COUTURE DESIGN

What exactly does couture fashion mean? More exactly, what is the definition of "couture"? According to the Oxford dictionary, couture means "the design and manufacture of fashionable clothes to a client's specific requirements and measurements". Essentially this is about fostering a new slogan: "Buy now, wear forever", which for example has been championed by Federico Marchetti, the founder of Yoox Net-A-Porter Group and chair of an initiative task force in collaboration with the UK on fashion. Yoox Net-A-Porter Group (YNAP) is the world's leading online luxury and fashion retailer.

Federico and his unique multi-brand of retail luxury ecosystem is revolutionizing and setting new standards in the world of sustainable, luxury couture fashion. He has turned luxury and sustainability into doable as well as trendy. This new way of couture design is pioneering the path for a way of building a responsible business that respects the environment and humanity without sacrificing luxury. In a recent article in GQ magazine, he explains "why now is the time to think differently about the way we produce, disseminate and consume our clothing".

The emergence of collaborations and partnerships between brands as well as professions is a path that will have a significant positive impact on the future of the fashion industry.
Recently, my brand label DoviArt signed up to work with a celebrity shoe designer for my upcoming show in New York Fashion Week slated for September. On a larger, more global scale, the forging of an alliance between Federico Marchetti and the UK to revitalize their fashion industry is opening up doors of limitless possibilities in the future for a new era of luxury and sustainable couture design.

This Anglo-Italian link is a shining example of the opportunities that are becoming available to the fashion industry in a reimagined world of luxury clothing. The collaboration has resulted in the creation of a project named Modern Artisan Project. Federico describes the project with the UK as a way of combining forces with YNAP "…to produce a successful luxurious label from sustainable textiles. This truly international effort involved a design team in Italy, a squad of British artisans based in Ayrshire, Scotland, and fused traditional craft with digitally infused creativity. The success of Modern Artisan is the marrying of these two distinct and separate elements." The project is a launch of a fully sustainable capsule collection designed by artisanal trainees. The "Yoox Net-A-Porter Collection" is a new capsule of some eight handmade menswear pieces, each having been designed and crafted by modern artisan trainees in order to – in the words of the retail group – "strengthen textile skills training and equip trainee artisans in the UK and Italy with the skills and confidence to produce luxury apparel to the highest standards". Designed by six Italian students from the Politecnico di Milano's Fashion In Process (FIP) course and handmade at Dumfries House – the headquarters of this initiative based in Ayrshire, Scotland – by six British craftspeople, all proceeds from the collection will go directly back to its essential Future Textiles program."

For instance, one of the most notable pieces from their collection is an ivory-hued cashmere rollneck finished with cable-knit detailing, which has been manufactured at Johnstons of Elgin's mill in Hawick, Scotland, where all of the aforementioned British artisans were taught the essential skills in the knitwear development process.

5. NEW STANDARDS IN COUTURE DESIGN

With regards to the rollout of their collection and the trainees involved, the UK representative of the foundation established to support the partnership and issued a statement that "Hopefully they will take away a great deal of skill and understanding of sustainable approaches to design and manufacturing that they can apply to their own businesses or future careers. The key is to rediscover the importance that nature plays, understand where natural materials come from and how they can be used in exciting and innovative ways. After all, nature is the source of everything."

After my own extensive experience as a fashion designer and laboring to build as well as inspire a forward thinking, higher purpose and conscious driven fashion industry, I had been feeling disappointment at the lack of urgency and now hope is renewed.

I am sure I speak to many designers out there who might be on the brink of giving up feeling as if they have been swimming upstream for so long.
May this chapter awaken a sense of "Yes, I can!" May it foster a renewed commitment to finding a way to be a part of such types of higher conscious movements of change.

I urge you to seek out and cultivate relationships with like-minded designers/manufacturers as yourself, build aligned partnerships and keep reaching out to see how you can get involved regardless of how small or large the project is. Remember: planting tiny seeds now will create that blooming garden in the future.

LUXURY OF THE NEW ERA   *DOVILE RIEBSCHLAGER*

Another trailblazing fashion designer who deserves mention here and who has left an indelible mark on the fashion industry is none other than punk pioneer and sustainable fashion queen Vivienne Westwood. She is known as the fashion outsider who rose to the top and has been at the peak of her game for more than 40 years. "Starting as an out-and-out punk, the designer became more mellow and sophisticated over time, but she's always held onto the ethics she started out with." And she has always battled the establishment. Despite her longevity in the industry, she has managed to always maintain a totally forward-looking mission. "Her company is run highly sustainably, avoiding the use of anything that's difficult to recycle, shunning the use of plastics and using recycled materials instead of polyester and acrylic. Sustainable leather holds a central part in so many of her creations. Vivienne, Westwwod, not long before her passing away in December 2022, partnered with not-for-profit organization Canopy in an initiative to combat deforestation."

Vivienne Westwood's Global Brand Director Christopher Di Pietro said: "Fashion has a disproportionate effect on the environment, and to remedy that we have for some time been changing the way we make clothes to reflect the need for the industry to change the way it operates."
In keeping with the values of her company, Westwood uses leather sustainably sourced from Maasai tribespeople in Kenya.

"She has supported projects in East Africa for more than ten years. Her 'Handmade with Love' bag collection has helped support thousands of people who were living in poverty.

5. NEW STANDARDS IN COUTURE DESIGN

The unisex collection, which features totes, rucksacks and drawstring bags, was created from recycled materials found in Kibera, the largest slum area in Nairobi. Working in collaboration with the United Nations and the World Trade Organization, Vivienne Westwood's production in Nairobi has stimulated the growth of ethical businesses and allowed locals to pursue an environmentally friendly way to make a living; and the initiative helped people learn artisan skills while providing them with a stable income."

Vivienne Westwood expressed her sustainability ethos and mission as follows: "We are one of the last independent global fashion brands in the world. We exist to do more than just produce clothes and accessories.
We use our collections, collaborations and catwalk shows as a platform to promote awareness and campaign for a better world. We use our voice to fight climate change, and to mobilize people around its impact on Mother Earth, Gaia, who sustains us all.

We know there is a contradiction between our activism and the industry we are part of. Fashion creates products which are too often disposable, and which – through their creation, distribution and eventual disposal – can have a disproportionately negative impact on our planet, its wildlife and people.

We know this and we know we must do better. We have been adapting the way we make our clothes and accessories over the last few years to reflect the growing urgency to change how the industry operates but, in this time of climate crisis, we must go further.

LUXURY OF THE NEW ERA *DOVILE RIEBSCHLAGER*

We continually challenge ourselves to make all our products with greater care for people and the environment, lowering our impact as much as possible. We push for a fashion industry that we can be proud to be part of. We are committed to strong, holistic action in the interests of farmers, artisans, supply chain workers, brand employees, our customers, our communities and all life on earth."

An article written by Harper's Bazaar editor, describes the legendary designer and her sustainability theme as one who "...touted the idea of sustainability in fashion long before it was mainstream. When her brand was launched in the 1970s, her punkish DIY approach meant reusing materials and producing less. Since then, Westwood became an environmentalist in her own right, and the brand's de facto manifesto has been "Buy less, choose well, make it last."

"The last time the label presented at London Fashion Week, the collection was reportedly 90% made of materials that have a reduced impact on our environment. For fall 2022, the total amount of lower-impact and cruelty-free materials amounted to 71%, with the brand forecasting the number to rise to 95% once it takes into consideration what's actually delivered to stores. Organic cotton, recycled cotton, cotton from regenerative agriculture, recycled polyester, recycled nylon, and responsibly sourced viscose are just a few of the fabric combinations used, with six different fabrics from the collection upcycled from previous seasons."

Both the late Vivienne Westwood and Federico Marchetti's are showing us how change can happen fairly rapidly in this post-COVID times.

5. NEW STANDARDS IN COUTURE DESIGN

The Anglo-Italian alliance has given designers as well as manufacturers breakthrough tools and opportunities to be the catalysts for cutting edge impact driven results in our outmoded fashion world. Furthermore, it is also providing consumers with better alternatives when shopping for sustainable luxury clothing.

And, it does not have to be a snail-like process as we are witnessing the emergence of younger generations who are committing to and are being groomed at this very moment to bring about the long-lasting solutions we have been waiting for: the betterment of all. He has thought of all angles possible and seems to be onto a winning formula of success for generations to come. This century has been given the auspicious term: the century of light.

That is what has galvanized me to be a designer that is boldly seeking to break the rules with my own design creations and inevitably we will all have to rise up to be those agents of change. Nothing short of bold innovators can be accepted at this point who are delivering results and that value the well-being of each and every human soul as if they were thinking of themselves and always keeping our Mother Earth in the forefront of their minds. And the fashion world is certainly not exempt and cannot escape this responsibility.

So, in whatever role you might find yourself within the fashion industry and if you are looking for inspirations and momentum to galvanize your actions in building a new, forward-thinking way of couture design, look no further, I have provided you with some great examples: Vivienne Westwood and Federico Marchetti.

The next step from here is to reflect on the questions below and ask yourself:

- "How can I be a part of these kinds of change?
- "How can I be a protagonist in contributing to the legacy of this new way of doing business in fashion and beyond?"
- "What kind of legacy do I want to leave behind as a designer, manufacturer and buyer/consumer?"

The new standard is when luxury, as well as sustainability, looks at longevity and helps the luxury brands to stand out from fast fashion. Luxury fashion brands ethos should foster deeper values of luxury that support social and environmental concerns and responsibility.

Moreover, you should feel good in them and let's even take it one step further, your health should not be at risk when you are wearing clothing. This is the elevated new way of doing business in couture fashion. The improved fashion system that contributes to the well-being of your children, family and future generations to come.

Here is what Federico had to say with the promise of a new future in the fashion industry based on his innovative invention and personal experience: "To deliver change at scale we must look to technology for solutions. Ever since I launched Yoox 22 years ago, in 2000, I've seen technology as a force for good. We are already at the point where we can avoid waste by analyzing data to predict long-term customer preferences.

5. NEW STANDARDS IN COUTURE DESIGN

We produce clothing incorporating digital ID chips which enable consumers to understand its provenance, as well as how best to care for and repair it, thus extending its lifecycle. The next few years will witness catalytic breakthroughs in technology to enable circularity in fashion.

And, of course, it's timely. Before the world ground to a halt in March 2020, the fashion industry was experiencing what I have often termed "global fashion warming". We were bombarded with shows and transient trends that encouraged a throwaway culture. And with "see now, buy now" – the industry's then ubiquitous catchphrase – it was no surprise to learn that clothing production had more than doubled globally over the past 20 years.

Jumping on the bandwagon, empty promises of sustainable fashion are commonplace, and every brand with a marketing department has a voice in the discussion. But unlike seasonal collections, which disappear after six months, we must ensure this current trend for sustainability outlives us all. In my own wardrobe, and despite the millions of items in the Yoox Net-A-Porter warehouse, my family will often smile when I pull out a linen custom-made monogrammed shirt that I've worn for the past ten years, or curiously examine the retro Fila Bjorn Borg tennis pieces I wore as a child that my daughter has now lovingly inherited.

Clearly then, solutions to the industry's crisis are possible, but they require the industry and consumers to come together under a shared vision of circularity."

So, what are your takeaways and a-ha moments that can propel you towards innovative inventions and as a consumer how do you see yourself supporting these types of initiatives with your spending habits? Any ideas come to mind? I hope reading Federico's story has opened your eyes to the limitless possibilities out there that you can either support and/or be your own version of impact in our fashion industry.

Even reading this book is a first step to being a part of this awareness and can even inspire through osmosis fresh ideas to highlight you as the catalyst for impactful change.

WHAT DOES TRUE LUXURY REALLY MEAN?

One must also keep in mind that luxury fashion can be a tough term to define. It could mean something different for everyone.

Luxury fashion could mean either of the following to an individual: a high price, exclusivity and uniqueness, high-quality materials, design, or craftsmanship.

As a result of these associations, and the assumption that people will naturally buy fewer luxury items than mass-market items, luxury fashion can appear as inherently conscious. However, is it really?

In going beyond just selling products, "these brands sell an identity, and consumers typically partake as a way to be a part of the perceived affluent elite. That desire for the appearance of luxury can sometimes outweigh the factual quality of so-called luxury products."

5. NEW STANDARDS IN COUTURE DESIGN

There are times when luxury goods are no different than mass-market ones. Some luxury products are expensive because the material is rare and luxurious, and the craftsmanship takes hours or even days. As in the case of my line of DoviArt clothing, every item is meticulously handcrafted. My ready to wear is more accessible but it is still in the luxury category as I source only the best materials and make every single pattern with the individuality of each client in mind and oversee every single aspect of manufacturing until the minute it lands in their hands. Additionally, I personally craft all of my designs locally in the US and everything is made to measure for the customer.

As mentioned in the earlier chapter, when I was producing the collection for the boutiques in Iceland, I had to source and produce them overseas, but I vetted every step of the process until completion. Regardless of how complex and challenging the process of sourcing, production and delivering it to the customer was, I made sure that I did not compromise on my values.

Let me share with you a personal story with regards what true luxury is vs. what it is not.

At this moment, I am creating and producing pant suits made from natural silk which I am including in my current soon to be released collection. The following scenario reflects how on the surface some seemingly expensive luxury brands are claiming high standards, yet they are no better than some of the mass-produced fast fashion out there as they are cutting corners and charging higher prices in the name of sustainable luxury fashion.

LUXURY OF THE NEW ERA *DOVILE RIEBSCHLAGER*

With the design of my latest collection around the corner, I have been researching some of the other natural silk suits out there and found out the disappointing fact that the lining is made from polyester.

Anytime I entered a store, whether here in the US or in another part of the world, and I read the labels regardless of their claim that they were a hundred percent silk, cotton, bamboo or wool, the second lining would reveal it was made of a hundred percent polyester.

You have to be a detective searching and digging through the labels as well as touching/feeling the fabric inside out. It is quite unimaginable that they are making garments out of the most luxurious, natural fabrics and claiming to be the best fabric out there, then one learns there is this unsustainable material, that we have been laboring to eliminate, being placed in the clothes trying to pull the wool over our eyes.

This nugget of information is for all you consumers so that you can take the initiative in reading labels more carefully just as you would pay close attention to the food you are putting in your mouth.

Your awareness and avoidance of the purchase of such clothes will be the reason for designers and manufacturers to take notice that their line is not selling.

Also, do voice your opinions by sending in your comments requesting a change to the brand headquarter office or directly to the designer. You can always easily locate their contact information online.

5. NEW STANDARDS IN COUTURE DESIGN

With DoviArt, I have made the decision that despite the current code of conduct amongst designers and manufacturers, the least I can do is to uphold higher values and standards. In this case, I have made a promise that my clothes will only be lined with natural and sustainable fabrics.

Right now, I am in the midst of extensive research to find which fabric would work best as a lining for my collection and I am considering one of the two, either silk or bamboo. I have dismissed cotton and linen as they wrinkle easily. Then, after careful consideration and despite the draw of some amazing wool silk blends, I realized I need to keep in mind current and potential customers who have very sensitive skin and have allergies to wool, the fabric that touches our skin. Fabrics should not be associated with any adverse sensory issues. They have to be very smooth.

The material has to be organic, no pesticides, minimum dye, natural dye or no dye at all. Just think of that polyester lining touching our skins and how when we sweat, we are absorbing the polyester into our skin and possible toxic elements that can be harmful to our health. Polyester breaks down with every wash, with every touch to your skin. Did you know that the average adult has five million pores on their body with approximately 20,000 on their face alone?

Pores are critical in allowing our skin to breathe and helping the body get rid of oils and toxins. Polyester is a manufactured synthetic fiber. It is a kind of plastic and is usually derived from petroleum.

Polyester has often been considered more sustainable from a consumer care standpoint – polyester garments last a really long time and require less water, energy and heat for washing. But a multitude of recent studies show that polyester sheds small pieces of plastic called microplastics with every wash.

These microplastics are filling our water and air, and are being ingested by marine life and animals and even us. While the full extent and impact of these microplastics is not yet clear, it is clear that the problem is huge (microplastics have been found all around the world) and could have detrimental impacts to plant, animal, and human health. Just imagine our million pores of skin cells absorbing all that plastic into our bodies.

My personal mission and commitment with all the clothes I create is that it always has to be about taking into consideration the health and well-being of the consumer as well as, at the same time, achieving luxurious sustainability: absolutely no compromises.

When I design, I am always thinking of my current clients and envisioning future customers by asking them: "How do you feel? How does the fabric feel against your skin? Do you feel good wearing it when the weather conditions change (e.g., when it rains, snows, wind blows etc.)? Clothes have to be wearable, functional, comfortable, luxurious and good for the Earth all together.
You cannot sacrifice one element for the other, thinking you can cut corners and short-change the consumer. That is true luxury and the new standard in couture design.

5. NEW STANDARDS IN COUTURE DESIGN

With DoviArt that is what I strive for each day, and I am looking forward to the day when every single fashion industry participant will be living by these higher conscious principles.

There is time and opportunities for designers, manufacturers, and consumers to step up and be active participants of a future where luxury fashion can represent positivity as well as strong ethics for our next generation.
What we need is more leaders to take bold action, break the rules and make it happen.

Ready to feel some more inspiration, invigoration, and like you can dress to save the Earth without foregoing quality and luxury? In that case, here is an example of a designer on the cutting edge of pushing the envelope with their brand.

ALLi BLAiR of New York is leading the clothing industry and doing it without compromising values as well as integrity.
They go by the slogan "where playful style and ethical living meets conscious consumerism".
Their mission is for each consumer to experience the joyful freedom of shopping without compromising their style and morals.
ALLi BLAiR New York (ABNY) is proudly introducing a path that shapes a sustainable future in luxury fashion.

LUXURY OF THE NEW ERA *DOVILE RIEBSCHLAGER*

ABNY is pioneering a new standard. ALLi BLAiR New York is the first company in the fashion industry that is claiming all of the following three facts:

- Offers only organic and recycled natural fabrics: works only with local, family-run businesses who manage the ABNY manufacturing in Italy. These are factories that they have built trust with, which ensures consistent alignment with their green manufacturing standards.

- Offers a 360°-degree sustainable retail experience from product to packaging to shipping to end-of-life: bags are compostable, packaging is organic and reusable, their shipping partner is circular and carbon neutral. Plus, they are working on a strategic take-back initiative with their fabric manufacturers and looking forward to establishing a vertically integrated fabric recycling program for their community.

- Offers whimsical, trendsetting, ethical clothing and accessories, proving that sustainability can be fun and fashionable.

- They are uncompromising with their production, never cutting corners and always making the sustainable choice. They proudly share their supply-chain, so that our customers can put their trust in them. Making the stand for luxury clothing without compromise.

Their powerful message is a growing trend in the new standards in couture design breaking down old, stagnant walls and building energy that empowers all stylish humanitarians as well as offering

5. NEW STANDARDS IN COUTURE DESIGN

a role to every member in the fashion community (even if you cannot commit to the life of a minimalist, at least there is an option for all you maximalists out there):

ABNY's mission is to "Make it possible for ethical fashionistas to find clothing that is vibrant, eclectic, and colorful. Clothing that they can fill their closets with, guilt-free and shame-free.

When choosing to be a sustainable maximalist, we want to make fashion available for you that can be worn for any body type, any season, any year, any decade. With the purposeful intention to make clothing that will never go out of style, you can hold tight to these clothes and love them forever.
ABNY clothing is durable to last for decades to come. While we hope that these modern vintage pieces will be passed down generationally, we ensure that even if they do eventually get discarded, the organic fabrics will not harm our planet.

Our manufacturing and fabrics will always be produced with the highest social and environmental standards so that you can be a confident sustainable maximalist, always."

A few other noteworthy mentions that are leading in this new era of sustainable luxury couture design are two Scandinavian fashion designers: Ann Wiberg's Trash Couture and By Signe by Rødbro.

As Vogue France put it best: Ann Wiberg's Trash Couture is "fit for an Urban Princess."

LUXURY OF THE NEW ERA *DOVILE RIEBSCHLAGER*

Ann's designs are mysterious, daring and sustainable which is what makes this vintage collection unique and has given it a cult status internationally. The brand enjoys an impressive following of A-list celebrities including Penelope Cruz, Kirsten Dunst and Kate Moss.

Established by Ann Wiberg in 2002, the brand uses stunning antique fabrics, laces, beads and unique embroideries for its creations.
The entire collection is hand-sewn within the company's own atelier in Copenhagen, thereby "minimizing the waste of materials and excess production, and ensuring good and controlled working conditions."

Another Scandinavian born fashion brand that was established in 2015 is the Danish design of Signe Rødbro, "By Signe is dedicated to creating honest and feminine easy wear for the independent and creative woman.
This is achieved through an honest design process that uses high quality materials while reducing the environmental impact during production. Rødbro started the brand in order to prove that apparel can be made exclusively in Denmark.

A truly remarkable achievement is that all of By Signe's clothes are made under one roof, from designing, to producing, all the way to finishing. This way, the team has full control over the quality of the brand's clothes and requires no complicated transportation costs. In contrast, other popular fashion brands often outsource their production, designing clothes in their headquarters, manufacturing them in one country, and then adding finishing touches in another.

5. NEW STANDARDS IN COUTURE DESIGN

As for its sustainability aspects, Rødbro felt it important to create something she could vouch for. By Signe's founder has a huge conscience and is well aware that the fashion industry is the top polluter in the world.

Rødbro explains that, contrary to popular belief, working with an environmental agenda doesn't make the creative process any more difficult. It actually makes it more grounded.

Thus, her brand joins the minority of fashion labels that ensure eco-friendly and ethical practices from start to finish. With its honest process and minimalist approach to design, By Signe has seemingly mastered the Danish concept of *hygge*. It is an idea that has no direct English translation.

However, some words associated with *hygge* include "pleasant atmosphere" or "cosy feeling." Over time, it has evolved into other concepts like "security," "peace," and "home welfare."

By Signe most vividly incorporates hygge in how the brand focuses on its clothes' warmth and cosiness by using natural materials like organic cotton, bamboo, and natural dyes."

These fashion designers are truly the ones to watch and I am sure there is much more yet to come in the way of meaningful contributions to our fashion world!

Now, if you are a designer looking for some great accountability markers for your fashion brand or are involved in the manufacturing/production end, you might want to consider investigating the B Corp and acquiring a certification through them.

The mission of B Corp is to "make business a force for good." B Lab is the nonprofit network transforming the global economy to benefit all people, communities, and the planet.

Their motto is "We won't stop until all business is a force for good". As one designer mentioned in working with the B Corp to achieve their gold standard B Corp certification: it is viewed as a designation for brands and for companies, that they are showing a demonstrable commitment to having positive social and environmental impact.

Being kept accountable to these best practices not only keep businesses aware, accountable and honest but also equip customers to make more informed decisions with a lot more ease.

POST COVID - THE PATH FORWARD TOWARDS RESPONSIBLE LUXURY FASHION

Over the past few years, we have been emerging from a state of quasi-hibernation and rethinking the kind of future we want to usher in the struggling fashion industry that is grappling to come to terms with the crisis it has found itself immersed in.
From a realist point of view, it will take effort and unwavering dedication, yet it can be done. Up to this point, I have described a few great examples of that light emerging and beginning to transform the world of couture design, one that can eventually lead to massive transformations.

5. NEW STANDARDS IN COUTURE DESIGN

What we need is increased collaboration, community involvement as well as investments of our time, money and energy.

Fashion is often said to both reflect and lead culture — the industry has a once-in-history opportunity to demonstrate that creativity and respect for boundaries can lead to authentic sustainability without sacrificing luxury in the process.

Covid-19 has been a catalyst for many things, but for the fashion industry it has accelerated demand for change. Consumers have radically altered their spending habits and that has meant that we all had time to contemplate the speed at which we consumed.

The Anglo-Italian partnership is a clear symbol for that emerging change and a role model for style – now let it be a launching pad for other emerging leaders in innovation that will also foster positive social and environmental change.

In Federico Marchetti's words: 'We must ensure the current trend for sustainability outlives us all."
As you read this chapter, my hope is that you and each member of the fashion community arises to start a movement and/or join a movement and to find one that is aligned with this new way of respectful, sustainable luxury fashion design.

What role will you play? What type of impact will you have on our world? I encourage you to start jotting out your vision board on these questions and as you continue to read through this book.

Then, take the necessary action and do whatever inspires you to take those bold steps in revitalizing our fashion world.
One that you will be proud to tell your children about and your children's children.

We collectively have the power to choose. And to change the system.

What is fashion? It is art and was born to respect the people as well as our ecosystem.

In conclusion, the following quote leaves a lot to contemplate upon:

"The system will collapse, if we refuse to buy what they are selling — their ideas, their version of history, their wars, their weapons, their notions of inevitability.
Remember this: We be many and they be few. They need us more than we need them. Another world is not only possible, she is on her way. On a quiet day, I can hear her breathing." — Arundhati Roy

You matter and everything you do matters. Turn your attention locally, to your community and attend to its needs.
Know that your spending habits, votes, and ways of living, and thoughts are affecting you and the planet.
You are empowered to make change. Pass it on.

5. NEW STANDARDS IN COUTURE DESIGN

Let's heal from the inside out, starting from whatever applies to our own health/well-being in tandem with collective humanity and our precious Earth that is crying out for help.
In the end, we are more in need of the Earth than she needs us.

How will you break the cycle and be a part of the solution?

KEY POINTS

- The emerging trend in couture design is summarized by the new slogan: "Buy now, wear forever".

- The new way of couture design is paving the path for a way of building a responsible business that respects the environment and humanity without sacrificing luxury. It can be doable and trendy.

- Contrary to past belief, change can happen fairly rapidly in this post-COVID times. We have seen the raising up of the capacity of designers (e.g., Anglo-Italian collaborative initiative) and manufacturers are being provided with breakthrough tools and opportunities to be the catalysts for cutting edge impact driven results in our outmoded fashion world.

- New innovations such the planting of digital chips in the labels of clothing to track the origin of the material is on the rise. For consumers, make the effort to start reading labels more carefully and if it is not up to standard, take initiative by reaching out to the designer, brand company etc. via email or write a letter. Remember, you have the power and collectively we can make change happen.

- Everyone in the fashion industry community has a role to play. The question is: are you ready to step up and what types of projects can you align with, support and/or create?

- We need more designers to make a commitment that, when they design their collections, they are taking into consideration the health and well-being of the consumer as well as at the same time achieving luxurious sustainability with no compromises. This is true and responsible luxury couture fashion.

What does Luxury means to you?

Am I as a designer encouraging to buy less cutting the branch I am sitting on?

Do you think luxury and sustainability are interchangeable?

Chapter 6
BREAKING THE CYCLE IN FASHION SHOWS

6. BREAKING THE CYCLE IN FASHION SHOWS

Picture yourself walking into a job interview and the first thing your interviewer asks of you is to strip down to your underwear or worse yet to stand completely naked. You also find out that a difference of one to two inches in your hip size is a catalyst for either your career success or failure. These types of scenarios seem brutally marginalizing, however for many models, they are facts of life. This is one example of a long-standing archaic cycle in the fashion industry and notoriously championed in global runway shows: unhealthy body image and the demeaning treatment of its models.

In an episode of "The Models," a Vogue magazines five-part docuseries, runway stars got real about eating disorders, size discrimination, and fashion's fraught relationship with weight.
Vogue mentions that "Fashion's unrealistic beauty standards and the below-size-zero samples often used by designers and showcased in fashion shows have made for a perilous working environment in which eating disorders run rampant and agencies encourage thinness no matter the cost."

To work under such conditions is to be constantly judged on your body. The pressure can be crippling, especially when it plays out in the spotlight. For instance, Gemma Ward, the Australian supermodel who began working in fashion as a teenager and experienced a natural growth spurt midway through her career, the comments about her appearance were akin to being "publicly shamed".
Ali Michael, who, at her lowest, whittled herself down to 98 pounds, had to endure news headlines and scrutiny about her deepest insecurities.

THE UN-GLAMOROUS VERSION OF FASHION SHOWS

According to the account of a former runway supermodel, Gabbi, mentions that "It's so easy to see pictures of models on social media and think they are living the dream, but the reality is most likely not what you are seeing. This is just a huge example of what you see on social media most likely isn't reality.

When most people imagine the life of a fashion model, I feel it usually consists of traveling the world, staying in nice hotels, making lots of money and just feeling beautiful and getting treated like a princess most of the time. Which, don't get me wrong, is partly true: some models definitely live that life to an extent. But unfortunately, that's just not reality for the majority of fashion models."

Gabbi describes what life was like for her in the industry: "As a fashion model, you are expected to keep your measurements at the ideal size which is 32" chest, 24" waist and 34" butt. It doesn't matter if you are 5'8" or 6'0" tall, anything bigger than this and you run the risk of losing out on jobs and your agencies dropping you. As a 6'0" girl, I can confidently say that it is impossible for me to have those measurements at a healthy weight… but this just doesn't matter in the fashion world. Agents will regularly pull out the measuring tape and make sure your measurements are in check.

6. BREAKING THE CYCLE IN FASHION SHOWS

I also had an agency in Asia that weighed the models every single week and wouldn't pay us if we gained any weight. This only caused my already present eating disorder to get worse and I ended up terrified of any weight gain. My agents literally clapped for me every week that I lost weight (even though I was under weight to begin with).

Then, I got back to New York City and my agents were praising me for my extremely underweight body. And my experience is actually mild compared to some other stories I've heard. I've had friends that have been told to stop working out, so they don't have to eat as much, to drink green tea or coffee instead of eating any snacks, and even to try out diet pills. Like I said, I could go on and on about this for days because I'm so passionate about how wrong it all is."

She goes on to mention that "… being in a career that revolves around your appearance is pretty soul sucking and it's the main reason that I decided to step away." The silver lining in all of this is that Gabbi managed to turn her life and health around. Despite her harrowing experiences, she can now proudly say that at the young age 24 (which is probably considered old by industry standards) she is a thriving health coach, eating disorder intuitive therapy recovery coach, and health/wellness influencer.

Another successful fashion runway supermodel is 25-year-old Bella Hadid (stepdaughter of the music composer David Foster) who is currently at the height of her fame.

For all you Instagram (IG) followers who avidly follow all the latest news in the fashion world, you might already be seeing your IG flooded with reels of Bella on the runway.

In an interview with Vogue, a new fact surfaced that the world did not know about and that is that Bella didn't dare speak to colleagues about the depression, anxiety, and Lyme disease, with an ongoing list of physical and cognitive symptoms, that have pursued her since early adolescence. She blames a habit of people-pleasing but does not let the fashion world, possessed of what she views as a "don't ask don't tell" attitude about mental health, off the hook.

Then, a few years ago "… on the first morning of New York Fashion Week she woke up and began to cry before her eyes even opened. She had already been working 15 days straight and, by her estimate, 350 days a year for the past seven years, and on that day she had eight fittings and three shows (an average day in the life of a fashion runway model). For the first time in her career, she backed out of her commitments. she believes that she had no choice — that her ragged nervous system could not have survived another fashion cycle.

"When you are forced to be perfect every day, in every picture, every show, you start to look at yourself and need to see perfection at all times, and it's just not possible," Bella says. "That month off was really helpful for me." Luckily, she is already at the top of the game and has the luxury to take the time off which might not be the case for a lot of other models. From this point on, Bella has made plans to say no more to the fashion industry.

6. BREAKING THE CYCLE IN FASHION SHOWS

Her lasting remarks, which should serve as a wake-up call for the dysfunctional fashion industry, is "Fashion can make you or break you. And if it makes you, you have to make a conscious effort every day for it not to break you."

Needless to say, every young impressionable young girl, who is insatiably gobbling up every social media news and print article of celebrities and the latest trend in what to wear, is unknowingly marred for life. They are unwittingly being molded into these puppets with a twisted sense of what a human and woman should look like.

A Gallup poll revealed that the average woman today feels as if she is 22 pounds over her "ideal weight," up nine pounds from 20 plus years ago. I would be very concerned as a parent who is raising up a young child in this day and age.

As consumers and if you are a parent reading this, it is my hope that you are instilling in your children such strong values and ethics that they will not be fazed by the glitz and so-called glamour of fashion, whether they are an aspiring model or just shopping for clothes and/or keeping up with the latest fashion trends.

The disheartening real life stories I have shared so far make one wonder how such things could be going on in this 21st century. It blows the mind that such an outworn and male dominated chauvinistic practice can still exist. Not only is the fashion industry, composed of everything from the ads we see in print as well as on TV to the catwalks of NYC and around the world, at fault for destroying our earth, but it is also the cause of illnesses, death and destruction of human lives.

This is where I feel the weight of responsibility and urgency to change the system. My opinion is that each designer as well as brand out there should be feeling this way, too. This is not just a fashion agenda, it's a human agenda. We all have a role to play in the well-being of our models, society, environment, factory worker and each other.

Whatever your role in the fashion industry (and yes, that includes you consumers) the key is not be passive bystanders or passive players in this journey of life.

To give us inspiration is supermodel Summer Rayne Oakes who stood up for her values and overcame challenges that crossed her path. In a Huffington Post article, she talks at length about her experience and provides the following insight: "What seems to be an impenetrable and immutable industry actually isn't. Granted that changing mindsets might be hard — and you might have to strip down to your bra and panties for the occasion — but character, confidence and fortitude always shine through."

Summer took an unlikely career path, she was able to parlay her background in environmental science and entomology with a successful career as a fashion model. She has co-authored the book, *Style, Naturally*, co-founded the award-winning materials marketplace Source4Style, served as a correspondent on Discovery Networks, and has designed environmentally preferable collections with Payless, Portico and Modo eyewear.

6. BREAKING THE CYCLE IN FASHION SHOWS

Summer describes her journey into the fashion world which started with these familiar words: "Your hips are two inches too big for you to pursue your dream in fashion." Unlike some of the other fresh, vulnerable and naive models, she had already years of experience in other arenas, from research in toxic organic contaminants in sewage sludge to mine reclamation.

She had been concurrently working as well on a project called Organic Portraits, a photo series published with photographer John F. Cooper that uniquely tied together the worlds of fashion and environmental activism. This initiative led her to a larger idea which caused her to reflect on and embark on a new mission: "Was it possible to use modeling as a platform for spreading awareness of environmental issues? And even more, could I use my place in the modeling ranks to strictly work with companies that share in my values?"

She goes on to recount: "It seemed promising but for a newbie, everything was so untouchable, so elitist, so entrenched, and unequivocally mysterious. There were a few good people and businesses along the way, however, that made me think it could become a reality. I even met models who shared my vision, including Angela Lindvall, Kate Dillon and Mak Gilchrist.

I was excited to share my ideas of bringing sustainable practices to an industry that seemed devoid of that value set. I figured that if I could work strictly with brands and projects that were making that vision a reality, we'd all be able to move the dial forward.

The agents listened to my big-picture plans, and at the end, one of them looked me squarely in the face and said, "Well, you know 80 percent of the jobs won't be available to you because your hips are two inches too big?" Which she laughed and said: "I couldn't believe that anyone who understood my vision could think something so superficial. I remember exactly how I responded: "If you think for one second that two inches on my hips are going to stop me from doing what I want to do, then you are sadly mistaken.

The fashion industry is filled with all kinds of people — some of whom have maintained the status quo and others who have the courage to shift it. The industry encourages models, agents and even designers to think inside the box and isn't used to embracing and cultivating what is unique. But while one agent, designer or brand may not see your vision, perhaps another will. I decided to take the risk to establish my own company and my own career. This of course didn't come without its pain either. I vividly recall crying in the corner of my bedroom in September (during fashion week nonetheless!) when the world seemed all too heavy.

There are still major issues and insecurities across the industry — from inequities around race to body image, but I cannot stress enough how these conversations and practices change when people have the audacity to speak their mind and say 'no' to working with certain clients. I only wish more models would do so (Abercrombie and Fitch, anyone?)."

6. BREAKING THE CYCLE IN FASHION SHOWS

DESIGNING AND BRANDING FOR THE AVERAGE WOMAN

Going back to the Gallup poll where the average woman today feels as if she is 22 pounds over her 'ideal weight', then, how should designers and brands be portraying themselves, particularly if more of their customers are, on average, bigger than what they were years ago? When models Summer and Kate Dillon were interviewed, they explained that "In the fashion industry when you are selling clothes, you want it to be about the clothes, so it's customary that you want the model to disappear. A lot of times they try to asexualize it to a hanger. It's harder to fit things to a curve and easier to fit clothes to a straight line."

Times have changed and women's sizes can no longer fit into the fashion industry outworn view of sizing effort, given that now the average woman is a size 14. The new way is the acceptance of a diversity of looks that celebrate the healthy image of women as just the way they are.

"It's fashion," admits Dillon. "It's important to keep a level of fantasy, but we both agree that doesn't mean it has to be a fantasy that intentionally harms a human being. We need a greater push from all members of the style community: advertisers, clients, designers, agents, models, media and consumers. As more leaders lead, it will get easier for followers to follow.

Though fashion can't take all the blame for all insecurities of body image that plague the world, it does fall into the sociocultural factor that influences women and the way we view our bodies. It is a part of the problem, but it can also be a part of the solution. If we have the chance to help and use our images and voice for the better, then we should."

Summer's advice: "The less obvious path is often the hardest. It's also the one, however, that reaps the greatest rewards. In the fashion industry, you have to choose not to objectify yourself if you don't want people to objectify you. I've made it known to my agent — and in turn, my clients — that I am far more than the sum of my parts. To models, I say this: It is your intelligence, your resolve, your character — your whole beauty — that distinguishes you. Don't shrink because it's what you think the industry wants from you."

An interesting development in England that might seem controversial to a few is the British clothing company Rose&Willard that is making it a requirement for their models to sign contracts in which they agree to not just eat, but to be watched while they consume meals. Should they not comply, both the models and their respective agents won't be paid. Even though it sounds overbearing, the intentions are there to make a change.

Rose&Willard's founder, Heidy Rehman, wrote an essay in The Huffington Post UK detailing her controversial, albeit monumental, decision.

6. BREAKING THE CYCLE IN FASHION SHOWS

"We have decided that we will include a non-negotiable contractual clause with the model agency which will state that the model must eat a meal and in our presence. We will not allow her to only eat a tiny morsel and/or suggest she'll eat later. The consequence of non-compliance will be that neither she nor her agency will be paid," she wrote.

The goal, she wrote, "is to provide protection for the models and their wellbeing. At Rose&Willard we are committed to protecting the models who work for us and are very much encouraged by public debate of this important and sensitive topic." Based on her own personal observations she mentioned that she had seen models eating tissues, and she said that many models she had spoken to said they thought they would get more work if they lost weight. She also discussed a model who was starving to the point that she had to be sent home — she couldn't function.

Rehman noted that she believes social media will help spread the word about her message. "We continue to believe that industry self-regulation is the way forward. We think this can be achieved by the public applying moral pressure to fashion brands. Social media, in our opinion, is the perfect conduit."

The question to ask is does it help the women? Forcing a model to eat under strict supervision doesn't exactly solve her problems, should she already have an eating disorder. Is this just a temporary band-aid? Perhaps.
What we need is a foundational and paradigm shift.

We need to be looking at all angles of this industry and as mentioned before there needs to be more than one player involved in this huge arena and we all need to be collaborating to support the shift. Doing it by force usually does not last for long. It comes with a change of heart and a need to see the importance of why we are doing it. How is the change going to impact our own lives for the better and leave a legacy behind worthy of mention for our future generations? We need to have a very important why to propel us into making these lasting changes. The hope here with this clothing company is at least they are trying to come up with some innovative, higher-conscious ways to be a part of the changing landscape of the fashion industry. However, we still need to do much more.

To give you another example, some countries have gone as far as taking drastic moves to protect models. France, for instance, has banned emaciated models from even stepping foot on the runway, according to a Reuters report. They need documentation indicating that they're at a healthy BMI. In that radical move, France seemed to send a larger message: that unhealthy models do not get work, and unhealthy is not something people should aspire to be.

How to Break the Cycle of the Un-Glamorous Fashion World

As a fashion designer, I have made it a point to always step out of the box and pick the less obvious path and I can tell you it has been filled with its share of challenges, however, when I call myself into account at the end of a long day, I know that I can sleep better at night with a much clearer conscience.

6. BREAKING THE CYCLE IN FASHION SHOWS

I have always made it my mission to understand, research and study the underlying psychology of this warped sense of body image as well as how it has been insidiously affecting our industry, and society at large and figure out how I can be a part of the solution.

Since WWII, we have been faced on and off with lean years as result of various recessions which required us to do with a lot less food and even starvation at times which might have something to do with the way it has affected people's mindsets. Traumas carried generationally tend to be ingrained and passed on unconsciously which can affect every strata of life (personal and professional).

The warped sense of body image that glorified anorexic looking models dates back to the Clinton Shields era in the 1980s — that is when the thinness image started to become more prevalent and was glamorized. Fashion runways and ads used severely malnourished models to promote their campaigns. There were even cases of some models dying during this time.

When you present a dying person in glamorous clothes and say this is glamour — people tend to follow and become influenced in their pattern of purchase etc.: a trend is set.
This is the easiest path of least resistance that most designers follow: they mechanically keep putting their designs on skinny, tall models and it is accepted as a normal way of doing business. Size zero is the winning ticket here in most runway shows and fashion ads.
Going with the crowd is the least problematic way of continuing to do business and design in the fashion world.

And, if you go against the grain and try to change the system you are viewed as a troublemaker and the repercussion is that no one in the industry will want to do business with you. Essentially, doing the right thing is frowned upon.

When I was starting out with my DoviArt collection and during my journey of presenting my designs, I pledged that I wanted my shows to be considered inclusion shows and that despite your body type you could still model. I wanted to stand out and break all the norms. At the time, I believe I was the only designer that pushed to use different size models to walk the runway.

I feel I developed this empathy and compassion to have this outward open-minded view on embracing the diversity of humanity when I modeled in Lithuania and was rejected. I know the pain of rejection and I do not want my models to have to go through it. I have chosen to never close the doors on anyone who wants to model my clothes on the runway, and on any other platform for that matter — I happily include larger size models.

The worship of being skinny and the ultimate pursuit of its perfection is a tragic flaw of our times. I have the power to be an advocate and the voice of change with my designs and who I use to showcase my clothes. I am interested only in showcasing healthy humans. Additionally, I feel that labels like plus size is also a negative connotation and I avoid using that term.

6. BREAKING THE CYCLE IN FASHION SHOWS

At one time, I lived near the downtown region of the city of Chicago close to all those high-end luxury stores, you name it, all the celebrity brand stores milled in that one section: Dior, Chanel, Gucci, Louis Vuitton and the list goes on — the area was known as the Magnificent Mile area. Sadly enough, I knew I could never wear any of those outfits and I was not even the heaviest woman around. Their sizes are not realistically made for real everyday people. Then, there are the designs that are produced in the factories in China. Most Chinese people have a petite frame. In production, it is not customary for them to sew for a taller and larger person.

From my experience, if you are not carefully watching the production process, it just does not look right when it is being sewed in the factories overseas. Production is being coordinated by starving and skinny people overseas and is not meant for the Western society per se. My plan is to be open to using models from all backgrounds, ethnicities, and sizes ranging anywhere from 0 to 30.

And I try to keep using the same models as much as possible. Typically, I will adapt the details of my designs to keep that visual effect and to fit my models.

The DoviArt luxury fashion line is about representing more inclusion of those who are professionals and look like normal, everyday people. My mission is to make beauty accessible to normal people. We are surrounded by nature that is full of life and color. Just look at the variegated colors of a garden — so many different sizes, textures and color.

LUXURY OF THE NEW ERA *DOVILE RIEBSCHLAGER*

In my collections I am always striving towards the goal of creating garments that are also full of life, color, boldness and one that embraces the diversity of our amazing humanness. When I advertise my clothes, I am also continuously keeping in mind the impact the images are having on the minds of the people, especially impressionable teens, young adults and women.

Moreover, I recently created a ready-to-wear line which was an area that was newer to me. I kept thinking when designing it that for it to be considered fashion, it needs to fulfill the requirement of wearability for the average person. When I go into stores with my friends all I hear are complaints that nothing fits them.

Then, I started asking random buyers how they felt about their shopping experience (including some of my clients) and they all echoed the same sentiments — there is not much of a selection to choose from, in these high-end luxury stores, that fits well.

Now, when I hear that, what comes to mind is that luxury clothes (that includes the higher-end ready to wear brands) is no longer functional and what is the point of selling clothes that are not wearable? Something else that stood out to me is that the clothes in these stores did not even have an area to accommodate the woman's breasts. Then, I also noticed that there's not enough space for arms, the armpits were too high and the sleeves too narrow. It is no brainer that when you design an outfit, you have to accommodate every single part of the body.

There is no way of getting around that and I can't even fathom what these brands are thinking. The customer needs and should be the number one priority.

6. BREAKING THE CYCLE IN FASHION SHOWS

No wonder the industry is on the brink of collapse, not only is it not sustainable, it no longer has any function either.

Even though breaking the cycle is not that easy, it is doable. This is a call to all of my fellow fashion designers to start being a part of the revolution of going against the grain. We just need the courage.

It has taken me the courage to make sure that my fashion is one that goes to the people, it has to represent the people — and I make sure I show that in even high stakes runway shows such as with any of my appearances in New York's Fashion Week. My hope is that the audience will connect deeply to what I am doing.

I want my models to represent something that is lovable and admirable, something positive. My advice to models: it is better to work on your inner self and your movement than to succumb to the pressure of conforming on how you should look to be perceived as beautiful. Inner beauty is more important than outer beauty.
I need intelligent women to represent my fashion. I want them to express their unique energy and cleverness? As a model, my question to you is "How do you want to express yourself and stand out on a crowded runway?"

Fashion that trickles down, has to represent the people. Let this chapter be a shout-out to all established as well as startup designers in the world. You have the power! Be the change you want to see in the world! It is never too late to start.

FINAL THOUGHTS

We need to address the decades-long system of undervaluing the nobility of a humanity for the sake of profit and outer aesthetics. Our efforts should concentrate on raising up the inestimable value that each of us possesses regardless of size and color. Let's take that gigantic step for man and woman — if we are to hope to create a blueprint for other industries to follow. Positive systemic change happens when we work together and act on our collective responsibility. My request to consumers (which I have mentioned before): when you buy decide which models and brands you want to support that are helping move that needle in generating impact.

Help to move fashion forward!

KEY POINTS

- Ask yourself what role do you see yourself engaged in when you think of breaking the current cycle in fashion?

- What can you do right now even if it is a baby step?

- How do you see yourself impacting the fashion world and society at large?

- Who can you collaborate with or reach out to in order to advance a more just fashion forward world?

- Recommendation for consumers: when you buy decide which models and brands you want to support that are helping move that needle in generating impact.

- Even though it requires effort, designers can be a part of the change revolution by going against the standard industry grain — by the way they choose to design their clothes and which models they hire.

7

Chapter 7
THE ENERGY OF CLOTHES ON THE CONSUMER

7. THE ENERGY OF CLOTHES ON THE CONSUMER

Have you ever given a thought to how the clothes you wear make you feel? The clothing you choose to wear determines your energy and how it can also possibly affect those around you. I am sure many of you know of the coined phrase: "You are what you eat", well, the same holds true for the clothes you put on a daily basis and that is "You are what you wear." What you wear has a psychological effect on you and has the power to change your emotional state.

In this world everything functions under energy. Albert Einstein summed it up perfectly: "Everything is energy and that's all there is to it." It is about matching the frequency of the reality you want, and which inevitably helps you get that reality.

When you project happiness and kindness into the world, you also tend to interpret things out there in a particular way... you then start to notice the good things in life. Your subjectivity shapes your world. The same philosophy holds true for the clothes you select to frame your body each day.

It is highly probable that you have heard the expression "energy is contagious". InStyle magazine states that "The aura is the energy that radiates and flows outside of your body. It dictates the moods and feelings that you have and affects the way you vibe with others. It can also transcend from person to person. In terms of fashion, matching your clothes to your aura can help you get on the right track personally, making you feel better about yourself while helping others to feel more comfortable in your presence."

My recommendation is to pay closer attention to your morning routine. Begin to ask yourself the following questions:

1. Am I throwing on an outfit without much thought as I rush off to work or to drop off my kids at school?
2. Am I present or wrapped up in a particular emotion related to what I have to get done today?
3. What is my mood today (e.g. tired, upset, irritable, sad, anxious etc.)

Remember your choices are strongly affected by your mood.

WHAT YOUR CLOTHES SAY ABOUT YOU

Most of the time, what a woman chooses to wear is heavily dependent upon her emotional state. Psychologists see a "strong link between clothing and mood and suggest we should put on clothes that we associate with happiness, even when feeling low. If your brain links Prada or Chanel's collections with powerful, intelligent women, you are likely to take on those attributes when you wear that Prada pleated skirt or Chanel jacket."

Human nature is to make an assessment of one another in the first few seconds of meeting each other.

7. THE ENERGY OF CLOTHES ON THE CONSUMER

The clothes you are wearing when you meet someone give impressions about your social aptitude, confidence and flexibility.

Your closet is worth the investment and should be given great importance as it can be a part of your overall well-being and success in the world. It contains so many options to boost your energy and it supports you in showing up as the best versions of your authentic self. It just takes a little more thought and getting out of your normal comfort zone.

Through my own personal experiences, I know everything is an exchange of energy.
One of my strongest beliefs is that there is an energy that is released into each outfit from the person who designs all the way to the factory worker who puts it together. If there is an unhappy, sad or negative energy when your item of clothing is being made, it permeates the fabric, and that energy will naturally transfer to the customers once they put it on.
To sum it up and put it bluntly, unhappy people will make unhappy fabrics which in turn transfers to the client and can affect their life.

For some, that might be hard to fathom but for the more highly sensitive individuals they can feel it right away. If you don't notice it at first, it might be as simple as when you step out with one outfit that morning and then come home for lunch, change for an after-work birthday party you will be attending in the evening and then, all of a sudden you feel this unexplainable positive shift in your mood.

Next thing you know: something delightful happens, you receive a call from a friend who you have been trying to reach for months and who now wants to take you out to dinner. Most of us would never bother to investigate the reason behind that. There might be a few factors and the fact that you changed your clothes can have a lot to do with it as well.

This positive change in your mood made room for an elevation in your vibrational energy. I suggest that you start to become curious whenever you try on an outfit, whether it is when you are shopping for one or what you already have in your closet. Make a mental note of it and if you have the time jot it down on a piece of paper (e.g. "This blue neon colored pantsuit made me feel….").

Reiki healer Kesaine Walker states that "energy's everywhere". However, if you're picking up on some type of emotion while shopping, the best thing to do is try the clothing on. It's possible that energy you feel could be from the fabric and even possibly, the store, the employees, or even other customers. You will need to develop that discernment skill and that comes with awareness and practice. It is like a muscle that is developed over time like going to the gym - the more you train and keep at it consistently, the higher the chances of your improved results.

"Tune in to what you're feeling while touching or wearing the items," she says, before sharing a few virtual tips. "You may not be able to touch while online shopping, but you can still tune in to how the items make you feel while looking at them."

7. THE ENERGY OF CLOTHES ON THE CONSUMER

HOW TO DESIGN AND CHOOSE THE RIGHT FABRIC OR OUTFIT

Personally, when I go into a store, I am always touching and feeling the fabric to get a sense of the underlying energy. I can immediately tell when some fabrics don't have the right energy.
It might carry a sad, tired or angry energy. At times, I have found it to be a challenging process to discover that fabric that carries that positive and elevated spark or vibrancy. And when I manage to find it, I purchase it right away.

I spend this amount of meticulous time to understand each fabric I am buying, because it dictates the design and ultimately how my client is going to feel when she wears it. My first collection was created in this fashion. In my search, I came across a section of silk fabrics in the garment district and ran my hands over it, and from there my DoviArt collection was born.

I cannot even adequately describe the experience of how it happened. All I can say it was magical and the inspiration for my designs were spontaneous and manifested with ease. I highly encourage each designer to invest the time and effort in touching every fabric you are about to create a design from and ask how is it making me feel? Is this something I would like to wear? Would my client like to wear this? If the answer is yes, then you have a winner on your hands and your clients will end up becoming repeat customers and easily attract more clientele that are aligned with your unique talent.

This is for seasoned as well as new emerging designers. It is so simple, just go out and touch the fabric, make sure you are touching every fabric before you buy it.

Furthermore, when I am creating my designs, I have found that a few established strategies (some might call it rituals) work well for me in embedding the right energy when working with a fabric: I express gratitude by thanking the fabric, the thread, the sewing machine for being in synergy with me, for helping me to realize my vision. Also, I always make a statement of love so that it's transferred energetically to the clothes that I am creating and, in turn, whoever ends wearing it will feel it as well. Our clothes can be sacred, and, so is our relationship to them.

I take it a step further by engaging boutique owners in a conversation about how to infuse the clothes they are selling with positive energy, love, joy and good vibes. I advise them to touch the clothes that are sitting on their racks and express their sentiments of appreciation and gratitude. It has been quite a transformational process for them as they mentioned to me that when they don't make that deeper connection with their clothes, the people don't buy them.
And, when they do, it sells. So, I have been told that they start their day by touching the garments. As you can see, there is this transformative energy phenomena that transcends the human mind. My counsel is that you start to become aware of it and consciously apply it in a way that works for you. Just the awareness can create those positive results you have been searching for as a consumer, designer and/or boutique/retail owner.

7. THE ENERGY OF CLOTHES ON THE CONSUMER

Stay tuned as coming up are some real-life transformations that I was an eyewitness to and will hopefully make you a believer that a change of clothes can shift energy. There's this expression 'the dress is wearing her'. This happens when you are not matching the energy of clothes.

REAL-LIFE STORIES OF YOU ARE WHAT YOU WEAR

Let me share with you accounts of how two clients of mine felt when they wore my designs. The first one was at a book presentation and one of my clients asked me if she could borrow a few of my clothes for this upscale art gallery event that evening. She was planning to have the girls who were working at the event and her assistant to wear them. After the event, one of the girls came up to me to thank me for letting her borrow my clothes.

She went on to state that she felt this great energy and was able to move so freely in her outfit. It was the first time that she noticed that the clothes weren't constricting her movement and how that made her feel as if there was free flowing energy in and around her.
Then, I received a call from another customer who had bought my clothes and she mentioned that she feels so elevated whenever she wears my clothes.

The latest example was when I was invited to attend the La Jolla International Fashion Movie Festival in California.

I was accompanied there with a stylist and her client Jill. I had the chance to dress myself, the stylist and her client.

When she came into my hotel room for a fitting, I sensed this bubbly aura about her but that it was constricted. Later after the fitting, I had a lengthy conversation with her as we waited for our red-carpet hour. I noticed there was some shyness and the stylist confirmed that she was quite shy. Despite our reserved and pleasant conversation, she kept lapsing into her quiet world. Next, after our conversation, she proceeded to change into one of the dresses I had designed.
I don't think I have ever witnessed a bigger transformation in my life than with Jill. She looked as if she was flying. She morphed into this ball of energy. All of a sudden, I started to see her everywhere, floating around with the energy of what can be likened to this beautiful hummingbird. The people were so attracted to her that they just kept coming to her to talk and get her attention. This change was truly extraordinary to see.

As we sat at a table with attendees of the festival, everyone milled around her — she was the life of the party, and she couldn't stop engaging with all those who crossed her path. And then she turned to me and said, "Oh my God, your dress just activated me!". Later, the stylist mentioned it was like this complete, 360 degrees turn in her character. Despite the fact that there might skeptics out there saying 'where is the science to corroborate all this?', all I can say is that 'you need to feel and see it for yourself' and, in my opinion, clothes have an indelible energy on you.

7. THE ENERGY OF CLOTHES ON THE CONSUMER

That is something you will never be able to get with fast fashion. Unfortunately, the harsh reality is that unhappy, underpaid people are manufacturing and selling fast fashion clothes. It is all about the profit and there is no soul in the process. When you speedily put together cheap, and environmentally unfriendly components, you can't expect to produce a masterpiece and great energy to go with.

Every small brand, every limited edition in the world, where there is that old fashioned process of bygone days, where the workers are treated well and are happy as well as take pride in what they are creating, masterpieces will follow and so will the energy that surrounds it.

That special infused energy goes beyond, you know, what you pay for and yes, to have that, you will probably need to pay for that higher priced label. As mentioned in the earlier chapters, it is about having less and then you won't feel like you are breaking the bank.

All it takes is to mindfully select the clothes you are buying and focus on a few high quality garments that can last you for years to come. Possibly even hand them down to your children.

PRACTICAL STEPS AND EXERCISES TO CREATING YOUR ENERGETICALLY ALIGNED WARDROBE

You will need to (as mentioned earlier) take an inventory of your closet. Do it on a day when you are not rushed or have to many distractions. It is crucial that you set a quiet, uninterrupted time dedicated to yourself in your room. Play maybe some relaxing meditative music before beginning to get you in a calm, grounded state, so you can actually connect on a deeper level to your own authentic energy and be able to read the items in your closet with more precision.

You might be thinking that is such a daunting task to have to take inventory of all that you have in your closet and how to best match it up to the energy you wish to project. The good news is, finding the perfect outfit that aligns with your aura is achievable and once you go through this process, you will reap the rewards later and it will flow so much easier once you have established that knowledge.

All you need to do is follow a few simple steps by picking the right color from your closet and leveling up your outfit in an effort for your clothes to be in harmony and aligned with you.
If possible, I would highly recommend consulting with a stylist and/or, if you are able to work closely with a designer that can customize an outfit for you, that would be an even better option.

7. THE ENERGY OF CLOTHES ON THE CONSUMER

For those of you that are not able to make this investment at this time, here are a few suggestions from stylists that will get you going.

- Divide up your closet into a work section, after-work party section, weekend lounging around section, casual time with friends section, and you get the idea — do it in a way that works for your lifestyle and daily/weekly schedule.

- Take into consideration the psychological impact of how you are feeling when you try on the clothes that are currently in your closet: does it fit with where you might plan to be going, and will you be in energetic sync with it? Maybe as you touch the fabric and try it on you are sensing a disconnect or a negative emotion which might mean you need to put that in a box to donate or recycle. When in doubt, just set it aside and come back to it later when you have more clarity.

- If you're ready to go out of your comfort zone and make changes on your image, subtle changes are the easiest and safest to make. Play with colors and accessories: layer colorful tops under your usual jacket, accessories can add variety to a look and accentuate the body in certain ways, little add-ons such as shoes, or sunglasses, or a belt make a difference. For instance, if you are looking to put together a polished and sophisticated image, you will feel systematically confident, act accordingly and people around you will perceive you in that way. Make sure you select something for each occasion and make a note of it. And, don't forget to keep touching and feeling everything you plan to wear. Keep observing your emotions as you do so.

A study from Northwestern University examined a concept called "enclothed cognition". Researchers define it in their report as "the systematic influence that clothes have on the wearer's psychological processes," meaning what your clothes are saying to you, not about you and how they make you feel. "When you dress in a certain way, it helps shift your internal self," explained clinical psychologist Dr. Jennifer Baumgartner.

Enclothed cognition gives scientific proof to the idea that you should dress not how you feel, but how you want to feel. Which clothes make you feel powerful? In control? Wealthy? Joyful? The clothes you choose are sending a message to those around you, but also to you, yourself.

Outfit choices are made to match mood and as a form of self-expression, but also clothing is used to control or mask emotions.

According to Mimi Raad, Image Consultant for an international news channel gives her tips for you to create a "happy wardrobe" which consists of wearing clothes that not only fit beautifully, but also need to make you feel physically good as well as energized.

- Remove things from your wardrobe with negative associations.
- If you are not able to part with certain item, lay your hands on the item for several minutes and visualize the old energy being released while you are infusing the clothing with positive and loving vibrations.
- Donate clothes that no longer fit.

7. THE ENERGY OF CLOTHES ON THE CONSUMER

- Stop buying eclectic items when shopping. Focus on outfit shopping so that you have clothes that co-ordinate.
- Detox your wardrobe twice annually – once per season.
- Buy only colors that flatter you.
- Don't buy outfits that are out of your comfort zone, you won't wear them.
- Focus on your assets and hide your weak points.

Keep in mind at all times, with each choice you make, that "Not only are we what we wear, but we become what we wear."

THE HIGHER PURPOSE OF FASHION

I live to design and through my designs at DoviArt, my mission is to empower my client and make their soul shine through what they are wearing.

That is why I design and my reason for the profession I chose. I want the person wearing my clothes to feel special, one-of-a-kind, someone, who stands out of the crowd and makes immediate and unforgettable impression.

What I show on the runway and in the boutiques that carry my line is the extension of my imagination and skill, but when I work with my clients, I listen, because it is not what I want, but what we create together. This is a collaborative energy we are creating together.

In my design consultancy business, I have made it my mission to guide my clients in their uniqueness and to discover the very best version of themselves. I am always providing psychological support in addition to my design services.

The DoviArt way is to always show in a new way and bring to light a new energy that is presented on the runways for normal people. Making high fashion that has great energy and is accessible to all humanity is what drives me.

Fashion should be about supporting and guiding you for your inner light to shine with the clothes that are customized for you. It is about your inner essence and how that comes to life coming through the clothes that are being custom tailored for you — a unique individual buying experience unlike no other. My hope is that all designers who are reading this will feel this responsibility to their clients.

As for consumers, you should not be accepting anything less than the best when you are purchasing clothes in a store or working with a stylist or hiring a designer to work one on one with you.
It is about your gifts and individual characteristics being brought out for everyone to see through the clothes you decide to serve as a mantle for your physical body.

I am always searching for ways to customize my designs that will truly embody your inside on the outside.
The goal of each designer should be about tapping into your soul and unlocking YOUR unique style.

7. THE ENERGY OF CLOTHES ON THE CONSUMER

When my models say that my clothes are comfortable, and that it makes them feel so good, flow with vibrant energy - then I have fulfilled my purpose.

In summary, that is the purpose of why fashion should exist: to elevate the nobility of humanity and their experiences in life and positively touch others around them.

Ready to start your new chapter in creating a wardrobe that has YOU written all over it? Well, look no further! Coming up are several questions you should set some time aside to reflect upon as well as put into action.

REFLECTION QUESTIONS & PRACTICE EXERCISES:

What are you wearing now?

....

....

Are you feeling sluggish or slow? Is the energy you are feeling connected to what you are wearing? Try to change outfits and check in with yourself and how that makes you feel.

....

....

Are you finding it difficult to get your brain into gear for this work task you're meant to be focusing on?

....

....

Have you considered just changing just one piece in your outfit to see if it can make a difference?

....

....

7. THE ENERGY OF CLOTHES ON THE CONSUMER

Can a different pair of shoes be all that it takes to shift your frame of mind and energy levels? Think of a few accessory pieces that might support you with that.

_____

_____

What is the one thing you have learned up to this point about your own unique energy that will support you when buying clothes from this moment on? What choices will you make in your purchasing habits starting today?

_____

_____

KEY POINTS

- What you wear has a psychological effect on you and has the power to change your emotional state. So, make sure to become more mindful and play closer attention to what you put on each day before you head out of the door.

- Matching your clothes to your unique energy can support you to build more of what you would like in life, and it will make you feel more confident as well as make a memorable impression on whomever crosses your path.

- Making the effort to invest financially in revamping your closet is well worth the benefits and results you will get as well as will ultimately outweigh the cost in the long run. Take inventory of what you have in your closet and purge what is no longer serving your higher purpose in life.

- Everything is an exchange of energy. Energy is transferred from the person who designs the outfit all the way to the manufacturer and the factory worker who sewed it together. So, become curious whenever you try on an outfit before purchasing it and make sure to always feel and touch it as well as take note of how it is making you feel in that moment.

- *As a designer, make sure you are doing the same, touching every fabric you are about to create a design from and ask how is it making me feel? Is this something I would like to wear? Would my client like to wear this? If the answer is yes, then you have a winner on your hands and your clients will end up becoming repeat customers.*

- *There is a higher purpose to fashion both from the perspective of the designer and the consumer. For the designer, it should be about empowering their clients and making them to shine from inside out. As for you, the consumer, you should be feeling comfort, flow, ease and vibrant energy as well as being a witness to your own transformations.*

8

Chapter 8
HOW FASHION CAN NURTURE YOUR UNIQUENESS

"Regard man as a mine rich in gems of inestimable value..."

BAHÁ'U'LLÁH

8. HOW FASHION CAN NURTURE YOUR UNIQUENESS

Finding your true self and nurturing it can take decades, and it might even be a lifetime journey for some of us. In a world where everything goes by in the blink of an eye and is immersed in superficiality as well as illusion, discovering one's true self can be overwhelming.

From the day we are born, we experience life through the lens of how others think we should act and, as the years go on, we are caged in these endless limitations. In our later years, we learn what it means to let go of our many false identities and go back to our source which is rooted in love and a spiritual foundation.

As your later years become a powerful journey of strengthening your unique soul's essence and purpose in life, we are led to re-evaluate everything in our day-to-day life. One of those being what we choose to wear each day.

Fashion legend Iris Apfel said in an interview with ELLE: "The key to style is learning who you are, which takes years, and there's no how-to road map to style. It's about self-expression and, above all, attitude."

The Gen-X age we are currently living in is characterized by who is "the next hottest influencer, Instagram and celebrity trendsetter, and the concept of embracing individuality has become increasingly relevant. Instead of dressing like someone else, finding a style that represents who you are is a powerful communication tool.
It can give you an identity – and on top of that, it sets you apart from the crowd."

Fashion and style should be raising up your vibration as well as frequency of worthiness and creating the expansions you wish for in your life. When a person puts on an outfit, she/he should feel beautiful and truly authentic.

For women in particular, we are greatly affected by the choices we make when selecting which clothes to wear. Our wardrobe has the power to make us feel confident, radiant, authentic and at the same time an outfit can dim our light or make us want to hide.

When you feel great about the way you represent yourself on the outside, you transform the way you feel on the inside... and that is your unstoppable confidence which will have powerful ripple effects throughout every area of your life.

More than that, each time you look in the mirror, the real version of you will be staring back, and you will feel like you're finally home: your true and unique self will be shining through.

THE HIGHER PURPOSE OF BEING A FASHION DESIGNER

September 2022 marked a new chapter in my journey as a fashion designer. I had the opportunity to showcase my DoviArt line in an 80's Punk Rock Revival show that I coordinated in collaboration with John Ashford Shoes which I have set up on a pre-order basis: they will all be custom made for my clients. This leads next to my thoughts while I was at NYFW on the importance of nurturing your individual sense of style and how fashion is such a catalyst for that when it is done right.

8. HOW FASHION CAN NURTURE YOUR UNIQUENESS

While I was sitting in the midst of the fast paced, chaotic New York Fashion Week scene, a sense of conviction washed over me as to why I am a fashion designer who keeps investing in this business. My truth is that I'm not in a fashion just to create another T-shirt, jean or another nameless piece of garment and make money.

Instead, I am interested in leaving a legacy behind for generations to come and my hope is that the fashion industry turns from being a machine profit- oriented business to being love-oriented and infused with a higher sense of purpose than to just selling clothes. For me, it is about my love for creating a design that people will need and adore.

Every minute I design, my whole heart and being is immersed in it and it flows out of an endless reservoir of love. I love the fabric, the tools I am creating with and there are times in the end (such as with my fashion show collections) when I don't know who is going to wear my clothes, but I'm sending my love to whomever will decide to order one of my designs. And, for that matter, this same principle holds true for clients of mine who come to me with special custom order requests.

The love I put into each design to bring out the uniqueness of each person stems from my own personal experience growing up in Lithuania, where I spent my youth agonizing about the way I looked and how I did not fit in even with my family, which made me search for ways to not conform. For instance, at an early age I felt that I was adopted as I did not look like my parents neither any other members of my family. I felt awkward all the time and kept noticing how my eyes, nose and hair looked completely different.

This experience constantly created this sense of pain in me, so I decided I would overcome it by using my innate as well as unique artistic talents to sew my own clothes. Also, I was rebelling in a way against the Soviet Union regime in the seventies and eighties where everything was uniform. If I bought a pair of shoes, every other girl would have the same.

For example, if I purchased a coat, the minute I would step out onto the streets I would meet, at least once a day, someone wearing that very same coat. I remember how women started using seamstresses to avoid this situation when they were planning to attend a party as it was not unlikely that a few of them would show up wearing the same thing.

For me, that was a huge pain point that catapulted me into the punk rock movement where individuality and standing out was everything. The punk rock movement had a huge influence on my career as a designer and the path I chose in life.

I am sure that each one of you has a similar story with different experiences. In a few sentences, I encourage you to go back in time and reflect on what was your pain point.

Were you able to overcome it? Have you discovered your true self and what makes you unique? What is your character brand? Grab a journal and make some notes.

8. HOW FASHION CAN NURTURE YOUR UNIQUENESS

TIP: After you write it down below, then set aside additional time to flesh it out in more detail in your notebook.

....

....

....

....

We all have a reason for being the way we are today and what shaped us as well as what we would like to be – being our authentic self. Going on to my "why" for being in this industry, it ties back to the previous chapter, where I touched upon the energy of clothes. My mission is to deliver clothes to have that special energy filled with love and care that will attract the right people to wear them as well as respect our fragile ecosystem.

My goal is to create that "je ne sais quoi" (a quality that cannot be described or named easily) – bringing out that unique energy of yours through the clothes you are wearing and where people will walk by you and say "Who was that?", as well as generate that wow factor where you leave them feel amazing and the best part is that you are grounded in who you are and holding true to your innermost character essence.

Remember there is only one of you and there are no duplicate masterpieces in this creation of life.

So, too, that is how I create my designs. I think of it as when all the planets align at the same time – the perfect synergistic harmony it creates. My vision and mission is to align my designs with the unique needs of the individual rather than to conform to society and just become a money making machine without soul.

Our markets are saturated enough with that type of mindset and there are plenty of copycats waiting in line (e.g., fast fashion). Clothes have the power to lift up our souls as well as empower us to illuminate all those who cross our path. I highly consider this elevated style and forward-thinking fashion which is slow as well as authentic and unique. If we see each other as gems of inestimable value, then as designers and manufacturers we have the power to change the face of fashion for millennia to come.

My challenge and question to you is what out of the box actions can you take right now to reflect this? As a consumer, how can you be an agent of change with your own personal style (keeping in mind not to forget higher conscious buying habits)?

On a much broader spectrum, this question can also be applied to all other participants in our fashion society from the designer to the manufacturer: how can you cultivate your own individuality as well as a higher sense of nobility with your creations and production processes? How can you be an agent of change from the way you dress all the way to how you are impacting those around you for the better? Take few minutes next to write down some thoughts/insights that might be percolating in your mind and/or perhaps take the time to think about it.

Then, write below what comes up for you as actionable goals.

....

....

....

....

EXAMPLES OF CULTIVATING A UNIQUE SENSE OF STYLE

Breaking free from uniformity and the pack can be confusing as well as challenging for many as we are all creatures of habit just going through the motions of life and fearful of standing out.
To give you some shining examples that might serve as inspiration, ELLE magazine asked the following women with unique personal style to talk about how they celebrate their individuality through what they wear.

Laura Hayden, a professional singer, stated that "Individuality means not being scared to do what feels best for you instead of what people want to impose on you. When I was growing up, I used to think I had to find one style and stick to it. Then I read an interview – I think it was with Kate Moss – and she was talking about how one day she wakes up and wants to be a sailor, then another day, she might want to go for a baby-doll look.

I remember thinking, why should we stick to one style?

Music is such a male-dominated industry and for such a long time I was trying to be one of the guys. I love clothes and I love dressing up, so now I've been dressing up a lot more and I've been enjoying that. If I dress up to go into the studio to write, it impacts the song. If I've gone in my gym stuff, it makes the song a bit sloppier.

When it comes to finding your personal style, I think Instagram is probably the worst place for inspiration. If it's on Insta, it's not going to be anything new or different, right? Recently, I've been feeling that call from mother nature to embrace womanhood, so I've been watching more films directed by women, I've been making a point of reading more books and poetry written by women. There's just so much out there at the moment to inspire us. We need to be free and unafraid to break the rules."

Zezi Ifore, a broadcaster and consultant, says of her individual flair and style: "I've always loved expressing myself through clothes. When I was a kid, I would change my outfit five times a day – I just couldn't help it. My mom is very glam as well.
She's a Nigerian woman who takes great pleasure in getting dressed, looking good and being her own kind of glamorous. That's definitely where I got my love of glam style from. She's always giving me tips on what to wear.

The most important thing style-wise is looking and feeling like yourself. It's not good to outsource your taste to anyone else.

8. HOW FASHION CAN NURTURE YOUR UNIQUENESS

It's a choice, and I really love it when people use that choice and look like themselves. I feel most powerful when I'm in tune with my body, my surroundings and, most importantly, my feelings.

My hair is also a big thing. No matter what I'm wearing, it means I feel like myself."

REFLECTION QUESTION:

What is in your wardrobe right now? Take an inventory if you have not done so already and see if you can find anything that stands for you and why you love to wear it? Do you even like the item? On the lines below make notes of what you observe.

....

....

....

....

If your clothes don't invoke in you positive emotions and a higher vibrational energy, then it is time to think about getting some new higher quality and good for the earth longer lasting outfits.

My tip is to connect with a stylist if you have the budget so they can work with you to elevate your one-of-a-kind style.

Another budget friendly idea would be to ask some of your closest friends to go with you on a shopping trip and get some feedback on how they see you when you try on some new outfits. After consulting with them — ultimately it is about how you feel — however, if you are unsure where to begin, getting feedback might be a starting point to get you going on your journey towards discovering the TRUE YOU!

Strategies to Cultivating Your Unique Personal Fashion Style

In order to be successful in both your personal and professional life, it is important to develop an image that is both authentic and conveying your distinctive message. The clothing we wear doesn't define who we are, yet it most certainly influences how we feel and that feeling is how we're perceived. Whether or not you decide to work with a stylist or a personal designer, what you can do at this moment is to embark on the journey of crafting your personal brand.

Mikado, a Los Angeles based team of stylists, here are a few of their recommendations:

1. ACKNOWLEDGE WHAT HASN'T BEEN WORKING

"Look at the relationship between the clothing you wear and how it impacts your state of being."

Each time you go out whether it is for work or for a night out on the town, 'Are you always struggling to find clothing that makes you feel like the best version of yourself?'

"Your wardrobe should act as a natural extension of who you are, showcasing your features and personality.
Acknowledging when it's not serving its purpose lets you know which areas to pay most attention to."

2. DETERMINE HOW YOU WANT TO SHOW UP IN THE WORLD

"Ask yourself how you'd like to be perceived by your clients, spouse, community, and anyone else you interact with. Establishing a description of how you want to show up in the world, provides the foundation for your unique personal style."

What would you like those first impressions to be about you?

My motto is to always nourish your creativity as fashion and style is a huge component of self-expression.

The next time you go out to shop, take this list of questions as it will support you in making better decisions with your purchases and always stop to think before making a hasty move:

- Are my standards and personality mirrored in this item?
- Is it inspiring me?
- Does my lifestyle fit with any of it?
- Where and how long will I use it?
- Does it match my closet with at least a few other items?
- Is it wearable throughout the year?

Now, you can consider making your purchase if, after answering these questions, the cost of the item is worth your investment.

3. EMBRACE EXPLORATION & DISCOVERY

You can't build your image overnight and with that you have to give yourself the time to play round, research and explore more about what is it that makes you who you are. It is all about trial and error, so that you can unearth the qualities that make you feel like you are the best version of yourself. The key is not to forget that you are always evolving, a work in progress, and… have fun with it. Adopt a light-hearted approach from your assessments to your shopping habits. The lighter and more energized you feel, the better the results of discovering your empowered sense of style.

MOVING FORWARD: CONCLUDING REMARKS

A few weeks ago, I learned of the news that Yvon and Malinda Chouinard had given away their company, Patagonia, to save our home planet, and their conclusion was that every business founder and leader should stand in front of a mirror and ask the following deep question: "What will my legacy be?" This is truly a shining example of how humanity can be of service to the planet and its people. This is so aligned with my concept that business should be based on love – love for our people and the earth.

Patagonia has been a long-time certified B Corp. I resonated very much with the founding principles of the B Corp movement. To give you a little history on the B Corp, the founders explain that "The original inspiration for the B Corp movement was a brand called Newman's Own that gives 100% of its profits to charity.
Thanks to the wisdom of other early responsible business leaders, the B Corp idea evolved to be not just about charitable giving, but about transforming the economic system through rigorous standards for overall social and environmental performance, public transparency, and legal accountability to balance profit and purpose. We are now seeing this evidence come to light on a magnified level by its commitment to its purpose of saving our home planet."

My deepest wish is that more fashion retailers and brands start to take notice of these types of movements and even consider becoming certified as a B Corp, so they are held more accountable for their actions.

I felt such respect and feeling real tangible hope for the future in the core of my being when I heard about Patagonia's decision. This hope extends to the possibilities and potential that can be galvanized in our troubled fashion industry. It takes a village, and we can be that village to make this type of change.

What a beautiful moment to signify the beginnings of regenerative leadership and how we can move into the next paradigm of custodianship, of giving back more than we take.
How can we redesign ownership structures to support regeneration collectively? This is how I believe movements are started and my wish is that the fashion industry takes notice and becomes a trailblazing champion of change. We all have a part to play in the collective whole and the question is who is willing to arise and move out of their comfort zone?

There has to be a willingness and readiness to stand out just as we would like to foster our unique identity when we choose our clothes. We are all part of a much richer and more dynamic tapestry. Dressing up to elevate our signature distinctive style is but one component to being a part of a larger collective change. Yet, it all starts with baby steps.

8. HOW FASHION CAN NURTURE YOUR UNIQUENESS

I hope this book has given you insights on how to be a force and proponent of change – shaping the future of our fashion world for the betterment of mankind and beyond. May it be an impetus for you to awaken to your highest potential in your remaining days on this precious planet of ours.

Winning business and industry is about acknowledging our inherent nobility, our oneness, and when we view each other as a united part of the whole, we can then redefine how success will look like for an individual and business, as well as give us the tools to become agents of positive impact.

It is time to retire these old, outworn methods which no longer serve or match up with the needs of our planet, people, and businesses. It is about asking how we are contributing to improving society and its overall well-being. How can we follow in the footsteps of Patagonia?

Won't you join me in reversing our fashion industry from a business of profit to one that is built on the basis of love and where sustainable profit is an inevitable result?

Goodness and love attract abundance whether it is in business or in one's personal life. This is the law of attraction and the way our universe works! My hope is you will say yes and join my movement!

At DoviArt, I provide consultancy and design services to guide you in discovering your authentic fashion style and supporting you to develop into the best version of you as well as providing direction and psychological support to live a life that you love on your terms. Nothing gives me more joy than helping women attain their highest purpose in life as it is not just about the clothes but giving voice and a platform to present the TRUE YOU!

So, if you are ready to give yourself permission to be all of you in your professional life, as well as in all areas of your life, and dress in a way that brings out your unique beauty and personality, I invite you to book a complimentary FREE Consultation Session.

KEY POINTS

- Fashion and style should be raising up your vibration as well as frequency of worthiness and creating the expansions you wish for in your life.

- As designers we should be creating clothes with the unique needs of the individual in mind rather than conforming to societal norms and become a money-making machine without soul.

- As a consumer, if your clothes don't invoke in you positive emotions and a higher vibrational energy, then it is time to think about getting some new higher quality and good for the earth longer lasting outfits.

- It takes time to build your unique personal style and with that you have to give yourself room to experiment, have fun when researching what makes you happy and explore more about what is it that makes you who you are. It is all about trial and error, so that you can unearth the qualities that make you feel like you are the best version of yourself.

- Fashion forward that is slow and mindful will require our collective energy and collaboration that reverses our fashion industry from one built solely on a paradigm of a business of profit to one that is built on love. Profits follow when the wellness of our global community becomes our top priority.

Want to learn more about my signature designing services?

BOOK YOUR FREE CONSULTATION

ACKNOWLEDGMENTS

There are never enough words to express gratitude and voice the words "thank you".

My heart's deepest wish is to be able to say thank you by reaching out to wrap my arms around each and everyone of you who had a profound impact on both my personal as well as professional journey.

I have now been given this wonderful opportunity through the pages of this book to convey my abundant gratitude in a way that will be permanently etched on paper forever.

There are so many people to thank and my list is endless and there is not enough space on paper to write them all down. What I can say for a fact is that life has been infinitely generous to me by sending extraordinary people to cross my path.

First, let me begin with saying thank you to Lorin, for being such an unconventional human being, forcing me to learn new things, expanding my heart and being patient with me, and working insane hours. You are my biggest inspiration.

Thanks to Loretta Petraitis for sowing the seed of writing the book. It took over the decade to bear the fruit, but time is relative to all things.

Thanks to Ilona Surgaile for remembering our conversation earlier this year, and when you made a very convincing case about my writing this book. You even took the step and introduced me to Denise Cumella. That was such a profound call to action.

Impossible not to mention Roma Šimkutė, bigger than life friend and couch. Thank you my friend. You were with me every step of the way, supporting, encouraging, celebrating victories, asking uncomfortable questions and pushing me to seek greatness.

And, I would like to end this book with my profoundest gratitude to my parents for the simple fact that I wouldn't have written this book if you two amazing souls had not met on the dance floor.
My late Father always encouraged my curiosity, always pushing me towards exploration and adventure.
My Mother on the other hand always made sure that I was safe on my adventures. I am here today living this amazing life because of you two and building the life of my dreams.

REFERENCES

(1) What is Fast Fashion and Why is it a Problem? Ethical Consumer
https://www.ethicalconsumer.org/fashion-clothing/what-fast-fashion-why-it-problem

(2) Fashion Transparency Index 2021, Fashion Revolution Foundation
https://www.fashionrevolution.org/about/transparency/

(3) Fashion; Two New Stores That Cruise Fashion's Fast Lane", The New York Times
https://www.nytimes.com/1989/12/31/style/fashion-two-new-stores-that-cruise-fashion-s-fast-lane.html

(4) Fast Fashion is Still a Big Threat to Our Environment — Here's What Needs to Change, Vogue
https://en.vogue.me/fashion/fast-fashion-2021-statistics/

(5) Style That's Sustainable: A New Fast-Fashion Formula, McKinsey
https://www.mckinsey.com/business-functions/sustainability/our-insights/style-thats-sustainable-a-new-fast-fashion-formula

(6) The Apparel Industry's Environmental Impact in 6 Graphics, World Resources Institute
https://www.wri.org/insights/apparel-industrys-environmental-impact-6-graphic

(7) The Global Glut of Clothing is an Environmental Crisis, Bloomberg
https://www.bloomberg.com/graphics/2022-fashion-industry-environmental-impact/

(8) Water & Clothing, The Conscious Club
https://www.theconsciouschallenge.org/ ecologicalfootprintbibleoverview/water-clothing

(9) "The Rana Plaza Accident and its Aftermath" International Labour Organization
https://www.ilo.org/global/topics/geip/WCMS_614394/lang--en/index.htm

(10) Fashionopolis, Dana Thomas

(11) 7 Reasons Why Apparel Brands Fail to Succeed
https://www.sgtgroup.net/textile-quality-management-blog/7-reasons-why-apparel-brands-fail-to-succeed

(12) Cotton Gin, Wikipedia,
https://en.wikipedia.org/wiki/Cotton_gin

REFERENCES

(13) Egypt Claims 30% Rise in Cotton Production This Year
https://www.fibre2fashion.com/news/textile-news/egypt-claims-30-rise-in-cotton-production-this-year-276777-newsdetails.htm

(14) Water and Clothing, The Conscious Club
https://www.theconsciouschallenge.org/ecologicalfootprintbibleoverview/water-clothing

(15) 30 Sustainable Fabrics for the Most Eco Friendly Fashion
https://www.sustainablejungle.com/sustainable-fashion/sustainable-fabrics/

(16) Reimagining the Fashion Industry by Designing Out Waste, Forbes,
https://www.forbes.com/sites/sap/2021/10/20/reimagining-the-fashion-industry-by-designing-out-waste/?sh=27f3d7b69e08

(17) Reimagining Textile production – The Source, Title PRESS
https://tittlepress.com/fashion/1523529/

(18) The Rupp Report: The Hall of Shame, Textile World
https://www.textileworld.com/textile-world/the-rupp-report/2014/02/the-rupp-report-the-hall-of-shame/

(19) Shay Sethi talks about the future of fabric recycling, Chemical & Engineering News (C&EN)
https://cen.acs.org/environment/recycling/Shay-Sethi-talks-future-fabric/99/i9

(20) The Pulse of the Fashion Industry 2018 – Full Report, Global Fashion Agenda
https://globalfashionagenda.org/shop/pulse-of-the-fashion-industry-2017/

(21) Environmental Impact of the Textile and Clothing Industry What Consumers Need to Know, European Parliament
https://www.europarl.europa.eu/RegData/etudes/BRIE/2019/633143/EPRS_BRI(2019)633143_EN.pdf

(22) New Research in the Netherlands: Synthetic Clothing Fibers Inhibit the Production of Lung Cells, Plastic Soup Foundation
https://www.plasticsoupfoundation.org/en/2021/02/new-research-in-the-netherlands-synthetic-clothing-fibers-inhibit-the-production-of-lung-cells/

(23) A Recap oF COVID-19, Supply Chain & the Future of Fashion Logistics, Fashinnovation
https://fashinnovation.nyc/a-recap-of-covid-19-supply-chain-what-is-the-future-of-fashion-logistics/

(24) How Global Supply Chains Are Falling Out of Fashion, Reuters
https://www.reuters.com/business/retail-consumer/how-global-supply-chains-are-falling-out-fashion-2021-09-30/

REFERENCES

(25) Fashion's Carbon Footprint: The Ins and Outs of International Shipping, Good On You
https://goodonyou.eco/international-shipping/

(26) Shipping is One of the Dirtiest Industries. Now It's Trying to Clean Up Its Act, CNN
https://edition.cnn.com/2019/10/03/business/global-shipping-climate-crisis-intl/index.html

(27) Fashion on Climate, McKinsey
https://www.mckinsey.com/industries/retail/our-insights/fashion-on-climate

(28) Fashion Forward with a Smooth and Flexible Freight Solution for Varner, Greencarrier
https://blog.greencarrier.com/fashion-forward-with-a-smooth-and-flexible-freight-solution-for-varner/

(29) Here's Why Made in USA Still Matters, Sourcing Journal
https://sourcingjournal.com/topics/lifestyle-monitor/made-in-usa-apparel-2-166871/

(30) Top 7 Benefits of Local Sourcing in 2022, Thomas
https://blog.thomasnet.com/top-benefits-of-local-sourcing

(31) **Federico Marchetti: 'We must ensure the current trend for sustainability outlives us all' GQ Magazine**
https://www.gq-magazine.co.uk/fashion/article/federico-marchetti-sustainability

(32) **Prince Charles, Mr Porter and Yoox Have Launched a Sustainable Capsule Collection, GQ Magazine;**
https://www.gq-magazine.co.uk/fashion/article/prince-charles-mr-porter-sustainable-collection

(33) **Positive Luxury: Shaping a Sustainable Future in Fashion, Alli Blair**
https://www.alliblairnewyork.com/blogs/news/positive-luxury-shaping-a-sustainable-future-in-fashion

(34) **The Most Sustainable and Ethical Luxury Fashion Brands, EcoCult**
https://ecocult.com/sustainable-luxury-fashion-brands/

(35) **The New Luxury: Sustainable Fashion, The Robin Report**
https://www.therobinreport.com/the-new-luxury-sustainable-fashion/

(36) **Redefining 'Sustainable Fashion', The New York Times**
https://www.nytimes.com/2022/05/07/style/redefining-sustainable-fashion.html

REFERENCES

(37) Polyester by Council of Fashion Designers of America, Council of Fashion Designers of America
https://cfda.com/resources/materials/detail/polyester

(38) L'Oreal Paris Faces the Facts About Pores, PR Newswire
https://www.prnewswire.com/news-releases/loreal-paris-faces-the-facts-about-pores-262699361.html

(39) Sustainable Fashion Brands in Scandinavia, Scandinavia Standard
https://www.scandinaviastandard.com/sustainable-fashion-brands-in-scandinavia/

(40) By Signe, Sustainable Danish Fashion, Future Positive
https://www.thefuturepositive.com/blog/signe-sustainable-danish-fashion/

(41) Vivienne Westwood's Fall 2022 Collection Celebrates the Art of Buying Less, Harper's Bazaar
https://www.harpersbazaar.com/fashion/fashion-week/a39124015/vivienne-westwood-fall-2022/

(42) Vivienne Westwood Launches Sustainability Initiative, Real Leather
https://chooserealleather.com/sustainability/vivienne-westwood-launches-sustainability-initiative/

(43) Ethical Fashion Series: The Legendary Vivienne Westwood, Numéro
https://www.numero.com/en/fashion/ethical-fashion-vivienne-westwood-climate-change-eco-friendly-fabrics-sustainable

(44) My Life as a Model: Choosing Not to Objectify Myself, Summer Rayne Oakes
https://www.huffpost.com/entry/modeling-industry_b_3287289

(45) This clothing company is forcing its models to eat, Business Insider
https://www.businessinsider.com/rose-and-willard-forces-models-to-eat-2016-2

(46) How to Develop Your Unique Personal Style, Mikado
https://mikadopersonalstyling.com/identify-unique-style-type/

(47) How I Found My Individual Style, Katie Frost, Elle
https://www.elle.com/uk/fashion/a28927773/how-i-found-my-individual-style/

(48) How Do We Find Our True Self? Zarrin Caldwell,
https://bahaiteachings.org/how-do-we-find-our-true-self/

(49) 7 ways to define yourself in your own unique way, Men's Fashion Magazine
http://www.mensfashionmagazine.com/7-ways-to-define-yourself-in-your-own-unique-way

REFERENCES

(50) Patagonia Asks All Business Leaders to Look at Themselves in the Mirror, B Corporation
https://www.bcorporation.net/en-us/news/blog/b-lab-founders-message-patagonia

(51) The Skinny of Fashion's Body-Image Issue, HuffPost:
https://www.huffpost.com/entry/the-skinny-of-fashions-body-image-issue_b_3308004

(52) Models Get Real About Body Image, Eating Disorders, and Size Discrimination, Vogue
https://www.vogue.com/article/model-doc-vogue-body-image-modeling

(53) The Not So Glamorous Side of Modeling, Gabbacado
https://www.gabbacado.com/blog/the-not-so-glamorous-side-of-modeling

(54) Why I Quit Fashion Week, Cosmopolitan
https://www.cosmopolitan.com/style-beauty/fashion/advice/a4745/why-one-model-quit-modeling-at-fashion-week/

(55) Starvation Diets, Obsessive Training and No Plus-Size Models: Victoria's Secret Sells a Dangerous Fantasy, The Guardian
https://www.theguardian.com/lifeandstyle/2018/nov/22/victorias-secret-show-angels-lingerie

(56) Bella From the Heart: On Health Struggles, Happiness, and Everything In Between by Vogue
https://www.vogue.com/article/bella-hadid-cover-april-2022

(57) UMN Follow-Up Study Looks Back on 40's Starvation Study, University of Minnesota Medical School
https://med.umn.edu/news-events/umn-follow-study-looks-back-40s-starvation-study

(58) Your Clothing Determines Your Energy, Rachel Hook
https://www.linkedin.com/pulse/your-clothing-determines-energy-rachel-hook/

(59) How to Align Your Wardrobe with Your Aura to Radiate Good Vibes 24/7, InStyle Magazine
https://www.instyle.com/fashion/clothing/how-to-align-your-wardrobe-with-your-aura

(60) You Are What You Wear? How Your Outfit Psychologically Affects You, Al Arabiya News
https://english.alarabiya.net/life-style/fashion-and-beauty/2016/04/13/You-are-what-you-wear-How-clothes-can-change-your-emotional-state

(61) Yes, Vintage Clothing Can Be Haunted — Here's How to Get Rid of That Bad Energy, InStyle Magazine
https://www.instyle.com/fashion/clothing/how-to-cleanse-energy-from-vintage-clothing

WHAT IS THE NEW ERA OF LUXURY IN FASHION?

The new era in luxury fashion as envisioned by Dovile Riebschlager has led her to become one of the most sought-after, award-winning designers in the world and she has been invited over the years by the prestigious New York Fashion Week to feature her collections.

The fashion industry is ready to step into this new frontier as shared by Dovile, where unchartered ways of moving into an era where fashion can retain its luxurious, glamorous status, and can also go beyond all the sustainability talk that has been emerging lately, are possible as well as achievable.

Fashion luxury is being reconfigured from old outworn methods and adapted to a new world in which the betterment of society is also rewarded alongside luxury and sustainability.

Whether you are you a fashion aficionado or the parent of a teen who is struggling to give him/her the best quality clothes or a seasoned fashion expert in the field eager to find out a solution to some of the pressing challenges that the fashion industry is facing today, there is a way for each one of you to be a part of this revolutionary change. Each one of you has an important role to play in this dynamic industry and can learn as well as benefit from Dovile's vast experiential knowledge.

In this book, Dovile shares her invaluable insights that will help you to:

- Stop buying poorly made clothing that gets tossed after a few wears.
- Understand the benefits of owning high-quality, luxurious clothes that will last you a lifetime.
- Save money in the long run.
- Implement effective tips to change your buying habits and wardrobe for the better good of all.

DOVILE RIEBSCHLAGER

Dovile is an award-winning New York Fashion Week (NYFW) designer whose brand was featured in the media outlets of the American channels: ABC-7, CNN, NBC, and other platforms. Her designs have been featured frequently on the runways of NYFW.

Her career began when she earned several degrees in textiles engineering and art. In the mid-nineties, life threw several opportunities to test her prowess and capacity as a fashion designer. Early on, she created stage costumes for a friend who was a professional ballet dancer and her troupe. Then, she tried her hand at commercial fashion design selling a children's fashion collection to one of the biggest Lithuanian apparel factories. That same year her first runway collection was accepted at a fashion show called "Woman and Fashion" which was judged by leading French experts in the industry.

From there, she went on to make her mark in the fashion industry with her trademark fashion shows and line known as DoviArt Fashion which is an elegant combination of art and high fashion.

Her unique and revolutionary creative collection incorporates a philosophical view on art and fashion. The DoviArt fashion line exudes an artistic rebellion and skill that comes from background in textile chemical engineering as well as fine art in textiles.

Dovile's offers private consultancy and works with clients by developing one-of-a-kind couture designs which are catered to their specific needs. She is known to tailor clothes that are made to measure upon request. She stands by her mission and promise to each customer: to listen intently to their requirements, and that the process of creation is not about what the designer wants, rather it is the spirit of collaboration, and what they can create together.

www.ingramcontent.com/pod-product-compliance
Lightning Source LLC
LaVergne TN
LVHW061045070526
838201LV00073B/5187